CHURCHES IN AND AROUND DAVENTRY

CHURCHES IN AND AROUND DAVENTRY

Ron Wilson

Foreword by the Right Reverend Paul Barber, Bishop of Brixworth

*t*roubador

Published by
Troubador Publishing Ltd
12 Manor Walk, Coventry Road
Market Harborough
Leics LE16 7BP, UK
Tel: (+44) 1858 469898
Fax: (+44) 1858 431649
Email: books@troubador.co.uk
Web: http://www.troubador.co.uk/

ISBN 1 899293 76 0

Front cover: Dodford Church, Northamptonshire

Printed in Great Britain

Typesetting: Troubador Publishing Ltd, Market Harborough, UK
Printed and bound by Selwood Printing Ltd, UK

contents

The churches

foreword
Right Reverend Paul Barber

For the past ten years it has been my great delight and privilege to travel round, and worship in, very many of the churches in Northamptonshire and Rutland.

Amongst them, of course, have been the numerous churches in and around Daventry, and it is excellent news that Ron Wilson has put together this new work about these historic buildings. With his faith and keen eye, he brings to our attention a wealth of fascinating detail in the wonderfully rich heritage that we share.

I believe that this book will give much pleasure, and open our eyes again to the great treasure that is all around us in the churches of this area.

Happy reading!

Right Reverend Paul Barber
Bishop of Brixworth

preface

Churches have held a fascination for me for as long as I can remember. My aunt lived in a cottage within the shadow of St. Botolph's Church, in the village of Grimston in my native Norfolk. The church clock, which always kept perfect time, was the guide for the day's events. I had no watch then! And I can also remember receiving a copy of a history of the church. As quite a young lad I was 'confused' by all the technical terms, and some of them still have me reaching for the dictionary. However, although these terms are important, it is the beauty and uniqueness of each building, which makes it special.

When I first came to Northamptonshire some 25 years ago, I was introduced to some fine churches in Everdon and Fawsley – and quickly got to know others in villages like Dodford and Newnham, as well as the two at Stowe Nine Churches. Since then I have visited many others in the area, and this book is the result of those visits. Some churches are almost like a second home; others are less familiar.

We hope that you will enjoy reading about the buildings, which are an important part of the Northamptonshire landscape – and which are still important in the lives of so many people today. Although there have been great changes over the last one thousand years, in many villages the only feature which hasn't changed dramatically is the parish church.

I am not an architectural expert, and enjoy churches for their beauty and for the atmosphere that they exude. However, we have given some simple explanations for some of the 'technical' terms to help you enjoy your visit to these wonderful buildings.

I can perhaps do no better in closing than to quote from *Welton Northamptonshire. A Sort of History* by Philip Goodwin. "You are standing or sitting where they have stood and sat. Some of you sit on their laps in the church in which they prayed. You or your children or grandchildren were, or will be, baptised where they received their names." A sobering thought that many thousands of people for countless generations have done just that; they trod the same chancel steps that we tread, and knelt where we kneel.

Unfortunately, due to vandalism and thefts, many of the churches have to be kept locked. It is usually possible to discover from notices on the door who holds the keys.

We hope that you get as much pleasure from this book as I have from visiting the churches.

In spite of all the help I have had, I am responsible for any errors that have crept in. In some cases I have come across 'conflicting' information and have had to make judgements about this.

Acknowledgements

This book would not have been possible without the help of many people. Some of these I contacted personally; others happened to be around when I visited a church.

I am grateful to the Right Reverend Paul Barber, Bishop of Brixworth, for writing the Foreword; to Graham White whose original idea inspired me; to Chris Nelson for providing me with a list of churchwardens; to all the churchwardens and keyholders who have allowed me access to locked churches; to John Smith (Flore), Paul Geldart (Church Stowe), Jenny Fell (Hellidon), John Buckley (Daventry, Holy Cross), Andrew Grant (Flecknoe), Jack Hobbs (Long Buckby), Gwen Darby (Lower Catesby), Philip Goodwin and Peter Mossop (Welton) and Pam and Peter Edwards (Woodford Halse) for their help and advice. And to Jeremy Thompson at Troubador Publishing, for his encouragement, and Alec Riddett for the time and effort he has given to the illustrations.

Ron Wilson
Welton
November 1999

introduction

Before buildings were erected for worship, people met in the homes of other Christians. In fact people were not allowed to have religious buildings. But Christians have always found ways of meeting to further their faith, and apart from gathering in houses, they managed to find spaces in underground catacombs where they were safe. Small chapels have also been discovered carved into rock, the best known example being found in Rome. This situation only changed when the Roman Emperor Constantine – who died in AD337 – became a Christian.

The first churches that were built very much resembled the well-known Roman basilicas, with 'adaptations' to make them suitable for worship. It was from this pattern that the excellent examples of Gothic architecture found in cathedrals came. Smaller parish churches eventually sprang up.

In Northamptonshire the oldest of these earlier churches is at Brixworth, but many other churches around the county, and especially in the Daventry area, also have interesting stories to tell.

It helps when visiting these buildings to understand how churches developed, and to know some of the 'jargon' when it comes to describing certain parts. The illustration on page xi shows the main parts of a church building. These and other terms are descibed in more detail on pages xii–xiii.

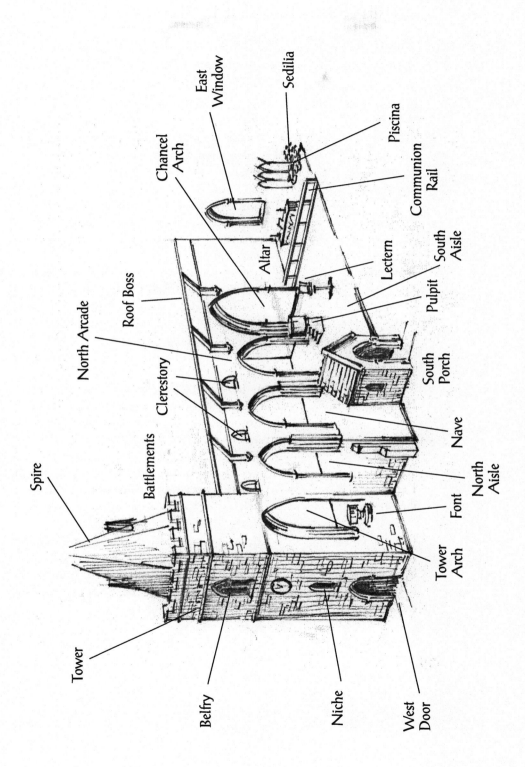

architectural and other terms

The following definitions of 'church' terms should help when it comes to looking at these buildings.

Abacus (abaci pl)	The flat slab on top of a capital.
Arcade	A row of arches supported on columns.
Aumbry	A recess in a wall, or a cupboard, for keeping the vessels used for Communion.
Ballflower	A globe-shaped flower with three petals which are arranged around and enclose a small ball – and from the 14th century.
Baluster	An ornate small column or pillar.
Balustrade	A number of balusters which support a handrail.
Battlement	A parapet that has regular indentations, and which is similar to those found on castles.
Bay	The compartment between pillars on a side wall inside a church or between buttresses on the outside of a church.
Belfry-louvres	The slatted openings in the bell tower.
Blind arcade	An arcade that is attached to a wall.
Buttress	Masonry built against an outside wall to support it.
Capital	The top (head) of a column.
Chamfer	Surface in which the square angle has been removed, usually forming a curve.
Chancel	The east end of a church with the altar.
Choir	The part of the church where the service is sung.
Clerestory	The upper storey of the nave which has windows.
Corbel	A block of stone, often carved, that projects from a walls and supports weight.
Crocket	Decoration placed on sloping side of spires, pinnacles, etc.
Decorated	Period of English architecture from 1290 to 1350.
Dogtooth	Small pointed ornament or moulding.
Dormer window	A vertically placed window in the slope of a roof.

Foliated	Design that includes carved shapes of leaves.
Fleuron	Decoration carved in the shape of a flower or leaf.
Gargoyle	Water spout coming from a parapet or tower, and carved in the shape of a human or animal.
Keystone	Middle stone in an arch.
Lancet window	Slender pointed window.
Lucarne	Small opening – often in the bell tower – to let light in.
Ogee	A double curve forming an arch.
Pediment	A low-pitched classical 'gable'.
Perpendicular	Period of English Gothic architecture covering the period 1350–1530.
Pier	A large pillar or support.
Pilaster	Rectangular column, especially one attached to a wall.
Piscina	A basin used for washing the communion vessels. Usually in the south wall close to the altar.
Poppyhead	Ornamental carving of leaves and flowers on the end of a bench or pew.
Portico	The centre-piece of a building with classical columns and pediment.
Reredos	Ornamental facing or screen of stone or woodcovering the wall behind the altar
Romanesque	Architectural style from the 11th and 12th centuries.
Sanctuary	The area around the main altar of a church.
Sedilia	Stone seats for the priests in south wall of chancel.
Transept	The 'arm' of a church crossing from one side to the other.
Transom	A horizontal bar across a window.
Vault	An arched stone ceiling.
fan vault	vault with ribs that open out into a series of elaborate curved fan shapes.
rib vault	vault with diagonal ribs along the groins.
Weepers	Small figures carved around the sides of some medieval tombs, usually representing the offspring of the deceased.

development of the parish church

The illustrations below show how, as building work became more common, the parish church developed from a very simple building to the more ornate and decorative types which we see today.

The earliest churches in Britain are of Saxon origin, and very few remain. Of those which do, most have usually been altered through the centuries. The illustrations below do not apply to a particular church, but are used to show how churches developed as additional parts were added.

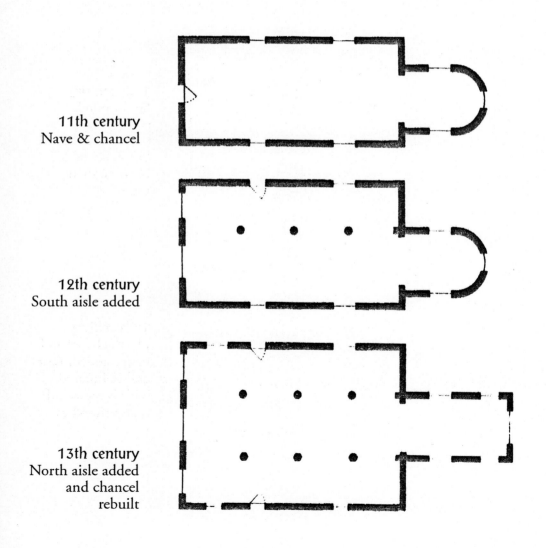

11th century
Nave & chancel

12th century
South aisle added

13th century
North aisle added
and chancel
rebuilt

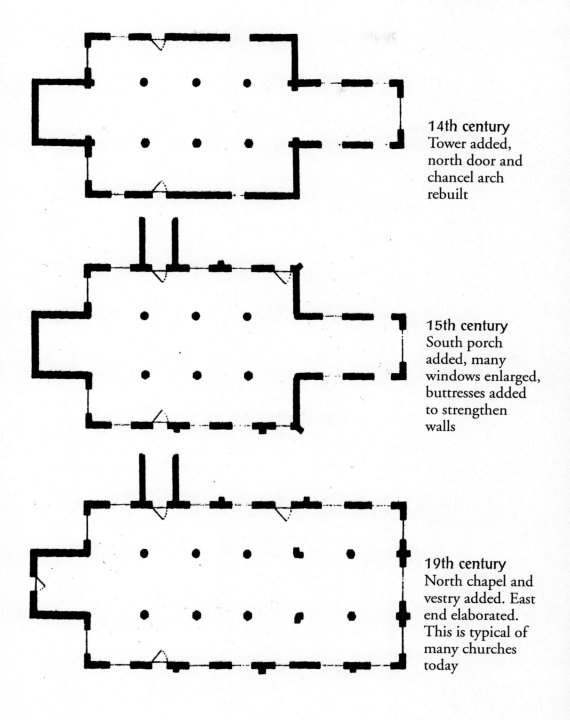

14th century
Tower added,
north door and
chancel arch
rebuilt

15th century
South porch
added, many
windows enlarged,
buttresses added
to strengthen
walls

19th century
North chapel and
vestry added. East
end elaborated.
This is typical of
many churches
today

adstone
church of all saints

L ike so many of Northamptonshire's churches, the Church of
All Saints is in a delightful position and situated along a country lane just off the Northampton–Banbury unclassified road.
Sited on the edge of the village, the church stands on a mound, and within
the shadow of the churchyard large trees – including lime, the ubiquitous
yew, and a very ancient holly – all add not only shade to this medieval
building, but give it an added air of peace and tranquillity. As with so
many small village churches, All Saints is well kept, with a neat, attractive
churchyard. The short path leads to the west porch, without windows,
resting beneath the bell cote. Small in nature, in keeping with the village,
the church consists of a nave with a bell cote at the western end, and a
chancel. Within the bell cote there is one small bell which, according to
Thomas North, was hung in the early part of the 19th century. Earlier
records tell an interesting story about the bells, showing they have had a
fascinating history. Records from the 18th century suggest there was no
bell in the bell cote, in contrast to an earlier account: "In 1552 there was
one bell and a sancte bell in the topp of the church".

Once inside, the south aisle, with its three bays and a timber roof lower
than that of the nave, dates from the 13th century. The chamfered arches,
with their circular piers and octagonal abaci, are relatively low. The
clerestory on the southern wall of the nave has three early two-light windows, which originate from the Perpendicular period,
and which throw light into the building. In the north
aisle of the nave there are two windows: the easterly one,
of two-light construction, owes its existence to the
Decorated period; the easterly three-light window is of
the Perpendicular style. The plain coloured glass, in tints
of green with blue around the outside, adds to the attraction of these ancient windows.

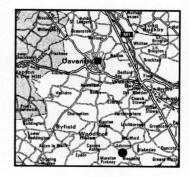

Significant restoration work took place in 1843, and
at the same time the chancel, with its slender arch that
links it to the nave, was added. The light coloured glass
in the east window lets in a welcome flood of light. It

was possibly at this time that the windows in the south wall, with their square-heads and three lights, underwent restoration. Further work took place just over twenty years later, in 1896. A closer look at the east window in the same south aisle reveals that it has survived since the 13th century.

Although there is evidence showing the possible position of a north doorway, which was probably 12th century in origin, and with a round head, it has been blocked in. In its alcove hangs a Roll of Honour to the men of Adstone who lost their lives in the 1914–18 war: a further tablet on the east wall also records the names of those who died.

The octagonal font has carvings of angels and other symbols, and also stands on an octagonal base, just inside the doorway. A delightful illuminated copy of the Lord's Prayer is on the west wall.

As with so many churches, the Victorians left their mark on the Church of All Saints, and here this period is reflected in the font, pews, pulpit and prayer desk. A 'box' which features some excellent Jacobean panels, and which stands against the east wall of the south aisle, has been a feature of the church for a much longer period, and dates from 1661, although it may not necessarily have been in the building for all that time.

ashby st ledgers

church of blessed virgin mary and st leodegarius

The village of Ashby St Ledger was recorded as *Ascebni* in the Domesday Book, meaning ash (*asce*) settlement (*bi*). This distinctive, beautiful church, dedicated to The Blessed Virgin Mary and St Leodegarius (the Bishop of Autun in France) – from which St Ledgers in the village name comes – is perhaps sometimes overlooked because of the other, often more dramatic events in the village in earlier times. It was in the Manor House, less than a stone's throw from the church, in which the Catesby family lived – and as everyone knows, it was members of this family who were involved in the unsuccessful Gunpowder Plot. Here in the upper room of the gatehouse, much planning is supposed to have taken place.

The church can be approached from many directions, but that from the A361 is one of the most delightful. The road meanders along the main street, with its many attractive buildings – thatched cottages vie for attention with old houses – a feature that gives the village its picturesque and characteristic charm. Undoubtedly considered one of the county's attractive villages, perhaps it is still haunted by the earlier goings-on at the Manor House.

Although rather slender, the west tower is the most dominant feature of this outstanding church. Built during the Decorated period (14th century), it is known that there was at least a Norman church on the site, because the Bishop of Lincoln (1186– 1200) indicated that the building should be called the Church of Leodegarius of Ashby. The present tower, supported by buttresses and adorned by battlements, has 'Y'-shaped bell openings with distinct louvres – the arrangement was important: it allowed the sound to escape, but prevented rain from entering! Hidden from prying eyes, the tower houses a ring of four bells, the two oldest dating from 1630. The third bell was added 11 years later, and a fourth was cast in 1806.

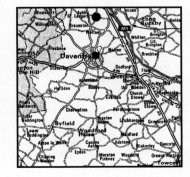

The gate leads into the churchyard, with its tall, elegant trees, making an ideal setting on the way to the round-arched south porch, with its stone seats and attractive windows, Once through the south door, the initial feeling is of spaciousness. The nave arcades are made up of four tall bays, which have double chamfered arches surmounting the piers with their double chamfers and octagonal piers.

It is possible that John Catesby was responsible for rebuilding the nave and both north and south aisles in Perpendicular style. The nave's eight windows, with exquisite tracery, are worth more than a second glance, and some have remnants of medieval glass. The stone work around the windows is worth investigating, too, for the many marks left by the original stonemasons as they prepared the stone. Masons also left their marks in other places, as confirmation that they had done the work and would – hopefully – be paid. There appears to be some indication that there was once an archway on the external east wall of the south aisle, suggesting that at one time there was a south chapel adjacent to the chancel. Further work took place on the chancel in both the 18th and 19th centuries.

The noticeable crest hanging above the south door might initially give the impression that it is a hatchment, but on close examination it appears to be the wrong size. It bears the inscription DEIU ET MON DROIT. It was the law that all churches had to have a royal coat of arms that indicated their loyalty to the crown. This one belongs to George III, and the white horse on the shield shows that he was a member of the House of Hanover.

Delightful as these aspects are, the undoubted treasure of the building is the magnificent collection of wall paintings. These first came to light in 1927, and they were restored in 1968. Characteristic of the artistic talents of our medieval ancestors, these paintings – a common feature of many churches – depict a variety of Biblical scenes. The earliest of the Ashby St Ledger collection is on the south wall, partially hidden from view by the organ case. Produced in about 1325, nearly 700 years ago, it shows the flagellation of St Margaret, with the torturer to the left, a whip in his hands. Those images that have been painted over the chancel arch, and which spill over onto adjacent walls, tell the story of the Passion. These

WALL PAINTINGS

At a time when many people were unable to read, wall paintings were created to encourage an understanding of the Bible. The paints used were equivalent to the distemper which, until recently, was used for colouring the inside walls of houses. At the time of their creation, distemper was made from lime water and skimmed milk, the colouring coming from a variety of natural pigments usually obtained from plants. Colours used included yellow ochre, lime white, lamp black and red. As the paint was applied to the wall it was quickly absorbed, so it was difficult to make changes to the designs. However, in spite of this the important feature was that once the paintings were in situ they became permanent. Having been a feature of many churches for hundreds of years, most wall paintings, together with much of the stained glass, was destroyed during the Reformation (the religious revolution of the 16th century). At this time, a way of ensuring that the paintings would not be seen was to cover them with whitewash. Any which survived this treatment gradually deteriorated, though many have now been restored.

cover the entry into Jerusalem, The Last Supper, Christ washing the feet of St Peter, The agony in the garden, Christ being nailed to the cross, The Crucifixion, and the Marys outside the tomb. These paintings all date from about 1500.

A particularly well defined painting of St Christopher can be seen on the north wall by the doorway. Since St Christopher was the patron saint of travellers, it was quite usual to have this in churches, and such images were often placed opposite the entrance. On the south of the west tower archway, time and death feature. Other fragments of paintings have survived around the church, including to the south of the west tower archway, the central aisle and above the arches. These contrast with the painted representation of a skeleton that can be seen to the north side of the tower arch, a fresco meant to mark the Black Death.

Although the wall paintings are undoubtedly the greatest source of interest, it is worth looking for some of the other interesting features in the church, including the Georgian box pews that can be seen against both north and south aisle walls. The nave features two very ornately carved Jacobean Squire's pews, and the three-decker pulpit, with its 18th century staircase, is also Jacobean. When this was used properly the clerk would sit in the lowest box, with the priest in the middle one, moving up to the top tier when he gave his sermon. Above the pulpit is a tester (a sounding board) that deflects the sound.

The tall, elegant rood screen divided the nave from the chancel, and is another of Ashby's remarkable reminders of the past. This was probably erected in around 1500, and might have been provided by George Catesby. At the south side is an old oak door, which would have allowed the priest access to the stairway so that he could get into the loft. It was here that the rood or cross stood, and it was from here also that the preacher delivered his words from the Bible. The panels were once adorned with pictures of saints, but these were destroyed by Cromwell's Puritans. Figures of Mary and John may also have graced this part of the church. The Jacobean pews that were erected in the 17th century have obscured part of the screen, so its full beauty can no longer be enjoyed. However, the screen is still a wonderful tribute to earlier craftsmen – spend time enjoying the excellent carving, crests, and the original colours on the lower panels.

There are three piscinas, one of which is against a pillar on the south side of the north chancel aisle, also known as the Arnold Chapel. The piscina on the south side of the sanctuary is from the 14th century. As with most churches, Ashby St Ledger has a number of monuments to well-known families. Some of the earliest of these are brasses, and that close to the organ is to Thomas Spokes and his wife Ellen. He died in 1416, and the single canopy brass shows the adults with four sons and twelve daughters.

There are also a number of brasses, the oldest to Sir William Catesby – who died in 1472 – and his two wives being found in the chancel. A further brass sited within the altar rails is to William Catesby and his wife Margaret. William fought at the Battle of Bosworth Field, and after he was captured he was taken to Leicester and beheaded. He was buried in Ashby St Ledger. William is shown wearing a tabard bearing the Catesby arms. Margaret exhibits coats of arms of both her family and that of her husband. The three sons and two daughters from the marriage are also shown. Margaret survived her husband by nine years. The full-length figure of Sir Richard Catesby (1553), showing a tabard with the Catesby arms, and in remarkably good condition, can be seen in the north aisle of the church, just outside the chapel. The raised pew at the west end of the south aisle had an earlier use as either a musician's pew, or minstrel's gallery.

> It was in the Manor House, less than a stone's throw from the church, in which the Catesby family lived – and as everyone knows, it was members of this family who were involved in the unsuccessful Gunpowder Plot. Here in the upper room of the gatehouse, much planning is supposed to have taken place.

Memorials in the chancel include those to the L'ansons, Ashleys and Arnolds. That to Brian L'anson, who was the first purchaser of the mansion, is interesting, as the inscription was not completed, and the date of his death is not recorded. The memorial on the north wall of the chancel, close to the east end, shows the two adults. There are also five named sons and five named daughters. The alabaster memorial to John L'anson on the south wall of the chancel shows that he died in 1663. It features a well executed three-quarter figure, and a medallion surrounded by a wreath, the garlands of which are almost obscured by a variety of heraldic devices.

In the 18th century further monuments were added to the church's collection, many of them to the Ashleys. That bearing the date 1738 is in the form of an architectural tablet with a crest at the top of what appears to be a small, strange bird. At the base three putti take the form of heavenly angels. Another Ashley – by the name of Moses – who died in 1740 also has a memorial, again in the form of an architectural tablet, and the roundel at the top of the memorial features his bust. Below can be seen the inscription, with the family crest also featured at the bottom of the memorial.

Victorian stained glass windows adorn the chancel, the east window being the work of 1829 craftsmen. It shows important events in the life of Jesus, including his birth, the Marys at the tomb, and the risen Christ. It was given to the church to honour the memory of Sir Joseph Senhouse. In the chancel's south window the glass is a little later, dating from 1850.

On the north side of the churchyard can be seen the door used by the family occupying the Manor as a short-cut to the church. On the south side of the church, and down some steps, is a memorial to the family of Ivor Churchill Guest, 1st Viscount Wimborne, Lord Lieutenant of Ireland, who was at one point Lord of the Manor.

badby
church of st mary

The delightful village of Badby has a long, ancient and interesting history, first being mentioned in AD 833. The present settlement, with its wide range of building styles and attractive houses, many of which are clustered around the ancient church, still retains its rural charms. Like many churches, St Mary's stands on a high point, where it overlooks, guards and protects the village and, almost within its shadow, the nearby historic Badby Wood.

Access to the church is either up Church Hill or Vicarage Hill, and both ascents are quite steep. Entrance from the road is through a gate, the path leading to the south porch, and in through the south door.

The west tower, originally built by meticulous craftsmen in the 13th century, is particularly attractive. It lost its crowing glory when the tall steeple crashed to the ground, though it was rebuilt in 1707. The tower sits on a mound, making it higher than the rest of the building, putting the west end of the church above the rest of the structure, which is held secure by a number of buttresses. The corners of the tower are enhanced with pinnacles, which support weather vanes. The tower has some interesting windows, including the double ones with Y-openings high up and just below the battlements. At a lower level there is an oval and a circular window, which are quite unusual features.

The sturdy bell tower holds a peal of six bells, three of which were hung in 1623, the others being added during the succeeding centuries: the last is relatively young at seventy years, having only been cast in 1932. This bell was added to the original peal when the other five were returned to Taylor's of Loughborough for renovation. Rehung in the same year that the youngest bell was cast, the rededication was performed by Bishop Norman Lang. Entry to the ringing chamber is through the small doorway, in Georgian Romanesque style.

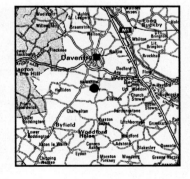

Once inside the building, St Mary's exhibits an aura of spaciousness and light, due in no small measure to one of the most striking features of the church's medieval architecture – the clerestory. The ten windows, in late 15th century Perpendicular style, are set quite close together. They have straight-heads with two lights, and are high in the lofty nave. This part of the church, almost entirely made up of glass, gives the religious house not just a well lit appearance, but also one of lofty grandeur.

The south arcade, constructed before its northern counterpart, is of five bays and perhaps at first sight seems less stately than the northern arcade. This may be due to the rather wider and lower chancel arch. Both arcades have octagonal piers and chamfered arches, and there are decorations on each end of the arches on the north arcade.

There are some interesting windows in the church, including the small stained glass one on the south side of the chancel, a 13th century feature. It shows St Cecilia playing a lyre, accompanied by St David on a harp. The inscription, of a much later date, reads, *To the glory of God in grateful memory of William George Warner, chorister and assistant organist of All Saints Church, Northampton. Died 14th November 1955, aged 44.* The east window in the south aisle was erected by brothers and officers of Major C. H. Uniacke, of the Scots Greys, who died on 30 January 1878.

The striking stained glass includes a variety of sequential Bible scenes – the baptism of St John the Baptist in the Jordan, the Nativity, Jesus in the Temple, The Last Supper, The Crucifixion, the Epiphany and the Ascension.

Perhaps one of the most impressive features of the church is the tall graceful 15th century east window with its three main lights, capped with Perpendicular tracery. The north chancel window bears an inscription to William Scratton, who served the parish as Vicar for nearly fifty years, and who died in 1919 at the age of 90. The window, placed here by relatives and friends and with the text *Lord, now lettest thy servant depart in peace*, is also dedicated to his wife Margaret.

There is a piscina and double sedilia on the south wall. The stained glass within the 1914–18 war memorial window has a picture of St George who, in this instance, has brought to an end the activities of a blue dragon. On his right St Michael, complete with flaming wings, can be seen thrusting his sword into a red dragon. It is worth looking through the plain glass partition that separates the bell tower from the main body of the church to view the west window. This is a well-proportioned example of Gothic revival architecture, and was placed in the church during the reign of Queen Victoria. It has some glowing colours in those highly dramatic scenes that record the Annunciation of Mary, the Mother of Jesus.

Apart from the stained glass within St Mary's, one of the other attractive features is the diamond panes of gold, green and yellow coloured glass in windows of the north wall. Although much of this glass is relatively modern, St Mary's also possesses some fragments of medieval glass dating from the 15th century. These relatively small pieces survive in the nave windows, and include a roundel in the north clerestory window, produced towards the end of the same century. To the left of the Victorian doorway, and on the outside of the chancel's south wall, a small square window has been filled in. The three-light window, which features a square head, is probably also the result of Victorian renovations.

In spite of being filled with light, one of the features missing in St. Mary's, but common to many other churches, is the lack of low windows in the aisle. Some of the chancel stalls are of a great age, and may have been in the church since the 15th century, and to these have been added more recent seating. The modern reredos, positioned behind the altar, has links with the past, as some of the panels once formed part of a medieval screen. Other interesting features in this well-cared for rural church includes a plaque on the west side of the north door to Frederick Bird, who died of wounds in World War I and was buried at Abbeville. The Worshipful Company of Glaziers restored the shields in the easterly window of the north aisle, and close by is an aumbry. A board of 1813 gives details of bequests made to the Sunday School by Sir John Knightley of Fawsley.

Like most churches, the line of priests goes back to the 13th century, and although we do not know when the first – Henry de Cokenato – began his ministry, the information board records that he served his parishioners until 1265, when he completed his ministry.

There are no large monuments in Badby, but a collection of smaller memorials taking the form of wall tablets, and which give an insight into past generations. Many are of fairly recent origin, mainly placed since the 19th century, and as with many churches there is often one family that dominates the memorials. In the

Another charity board refers to the Charity of Thomas Coles of 1733, who gave some land, the rent from which was to be used for the poor. It was envisaged by the benefactor that it would be enough to buy six threepenny loaves of household bread every week of the year to be distributed on Sundays at the end of divine service… amongst all such aged, poor, impotent, poor person only living and residing in town and parish of Daventry. *Such people could only receive the bread* who do not receive collection from said parish. *The people had to live* in the town and parish of Badby, *and must not be in receipt of other collections from the parish.*

case of Badby it is the Green family, who are remembered in the chancel. Both Thomas Green Senior and Thomas Green Junior are included – the former, who died aged 83, was the Vicar of Badby with Newnham for 55 years. His wife, Mary-Ann, is also commemorated on the same memorial, and the son, also called Thomas, died when he was only six years of age. The memorial to Thomas Green Junior is on the south wall of the chancel, and the inscription reads *To the sacred memory of Thomas Green, Esquire, BA late of Spring Grove, Isleworth, of the Inner Temple, Barrister of Law, and the eldest son of the late Rev Thomas Green. MA who departed this life on 24 May 1874 aged 53 years.* Another memorial is in remembrance of Major John Francis Green, born on 8 December 1856, and died on 12 December 1887 at the age of 31. He was the second son of the late Thomas Green, Barrister of Law.

blakesley
church st mary

The thriving village of Blakesley, with quiet, almost dream-like qualities, still retains many of its charms, including its distinctive village green outside the school. The church is sited on one of the village streets surrounded and protected by – and also itself protecting – the neighbouring buildings with their distinctive ironstone stonework.

The parish of Blakesley was constituted some time between 1147 and 1167, when Robert de Cheney was Bishop of Lincoln, though there are no recorded vicars until 1275, when Will de Melcheburn was installed. The parish passed to the Order of the Knights of St John of Jerusalem, who were Lords of the Manor. Walking up the short pathway from the street, the summer visitor is met by an array of roses and lavender, and there is a well-placed seat just outside the porch. Here it is possible to just pass the time, reflect on the history of worship today and over the centuries, or simply to appreciate the scents from the churchyard flowers.

Without doubt the most dominant feature of the church is the Decorated west tower, which dates from 1300. Whereas the rest of the church, like the surrounding buildings, is mainly of ironstone construction, this part of the building has been constructed from rough grey blocks. There are four bell openings, all with similar two-pointed trefoiled lights. The tower houses a ring of five bells, the oldest of which is the Priest's bell dating from 1552. At this time there was four bells and a sanctus bell. Renovation and re-casting has undoubtedly taken place over the centuries, and later dates can be found on the bells. Two are inscribed 1653, a third 1673, and two others are from 1854, with the older priest's bell of 1777 vintage.

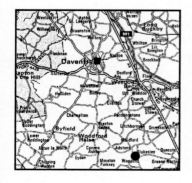

Apart from the striking nature of the tower, this attractive parish church also possesses another external feature worth more than a second glance. The nave roof is enhanced by the addition of some extremely well executed Perpendicular battlements.

Entry to the Church of St Mary is through the south

doorway into a spacious and open building. Once inside, just pause, gaze and wonder at the craftsmanship within this house of prayer. The building is in Early English (late Perpendicular) style, with the main body of the church being built in 1275. The original nave had a steep roof, and the line of this can be seen on the west wall. The arch inside the tower – which is not central – has triple responds, with half pillars attached to the wall to support the arch.

Both north and south aisles, together with the clerestory, were added at a later date. There are four windows on either side, and in both aisles the three bays each consist of Decorated arches, all with quadrant mouldings and adorned with distinctively carved corbel heads at the top of each capital. The clerestory windows also date from the Decorated period. An upward gaze shows that a series of bosses support the roof, where carved angels make music.

As with many other churches, restoration work took place in the 19th century, and the building was restored in 1873, though the chancel was not included in this. This was rebuilt towards the end of the 19th century, by the architect Edmund Law, with money provided by a Mr C. W. Bartholomew as a memorial to his father. A gallery that was built against the west tower wall in 1752 had a relatively short life, being removed less than a hundred years later during the restoration work.

The southern chapel, in late Perpendicular style, was built using money from a bequest made to the church in about 1500. The chapel is separated from the chancel by arches which are enhanced by elegant mouldings that continue along its whole length. The windows in this part of the church all have straight heads. Once referred to as St Anne's Chapel (Anne was the mother of the Virgin Mary), it is now the south chantrey chapel, and today it is known as the Foxley Chapel. There is a small statuette of the Madonna here, given to the church by Canon Capron to mark his retirement as Vicar in 1970.

In the east window, given in memory of William and Elizabeth Whitton, the stained glass includes a number of Biblical characters and scenes. It is possible to pick out the Blessed Virgin Mary at the Nativity, and Our Lord shown at his Crucifixion. Below this is an alabaster reredos

showing the Last Supper, with the Creed, Lord's Prayer and Ten Commandments on either side. The north and south windows have a representation of the Incarnation, and the stained glass window in the belfry, in memory of C. W. Bartholomew of Blakesley Hall, depicts faith, hope and charity.

Of the memorials in the church, the historical brass on the west wall is undoubtedly one of the most interesting. Dated 1416, it has a Latin inscription which, when translated, provides this fascinating information: *Here lies Matthew Swetenham, formally bearer of the bow and Esquire of the most illustrious King Henry IV who died on 29th day of the month of December in the year of our Lord 1416 to whose soul may God be merciful.* The figure, resplendent in a plain, but well executed, suit of plate armour is 3 foot 2 inches (105cm) long. At his left side there is a sword, at his right a misericorde. His hands are held in prayer, and his feet rest on a lion. The figure wears an SS collar, indicating that Swetenham fought for the Lancastrians. A list of vicars shows that Sir John Swetenham was Vicar of Blakesley from 1505–07.

One of the most intriguing treasures of this church is an interesting wooden sculpture of a pelican that hangs close to the nave roof, high up on the wall of the tower, just above the arch. Carved in medieval times, the pelican was a symbol of piety. The detail on the carving – which is not too easy to see from ground level – shows a pelican feeding its young with her own blood.

Another memorial of note is the hanging alabaster and firestone monument in the chancel, which has unfortunately been damaged. It now features four kneeling headless figures arranged in two rows. The inscription beneath the memorial indicates that is was to Mr W. Wattes of Blaxlye (Blakesley), a former Lord of the Manor, who died on 16 June 1614.

Other aspects of interest include a tablet close the belfry in memory of those who gave their lives in the 1914–18 and 1939–45 wars. Unusually, the church registers go all the way back to the year 1538. The screen which is the tower arch was erected as a memorial to Rev. Robinson, vicar of Blakesley for a short period between 1946 and 1949. The octagonal font was added to the church furnishings in 1874, when restoration work was carried out. It was a gift from the Rev. Arthur Hibbit.

braunston
church of all saints

The village of Braunston has a long history, but it was the arrival of the canal that made it even busier when it acquired the unofficial title of the "most important transhipment port in the Midlands", if not the country. With this new-found industry, and its accompanying wealth, there was a large influx of people to the community. The earlier church, mainly dating from the 15th century, was no longer large enough for this growing population. The inspiration for a new church in 1848 came primarily from the Rector, Rev. A. B. Clough, a Fellow of Jesus College, Oxford, who set up a fund for rebuilding. The church had long been neglected – not only was the spire leaning at an unsafe angle, but much of the fabric of the building was crumbling. Apart from its unsound condition, it was also considered that, with its maximum seating capacity of 363, it would not be large enough, and in the appeal literature the figures from the 1841 census of 1469 inhabitants was used.

As the building had clearly been neglected for some time, it was agreed to demolish it. This took place in 1848, before work began on the present building. In 1849 Birmingham architect R. C. Hussey was commissioned, and designed the present building. In planning the new All Saints, Hussey enlarged the building to make a bigger replica of the church that it was to replace. The Rector also included in the architect's brief the proviso that the nave should be large enough to seat all those pupils who attended Braunston's National School. This was at the other end of the High Street, and is now the village hall. The new church was completed at a cost of £6800.

Stone from the earlier 14th century building was used in the construction of the present church. In addition, the new church also used attractive Warwickshire sandstone, with limestone dressings, giving the building a warm feeling. The church has many attractive decorative features, not least of which are the ornately executed pinnacles. In addition to the 14th century church there was a Norman structure, and possibly an earlier wooden

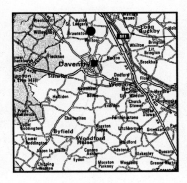

building existed before the more substantial church. The earliest of the stone structures, however, goes back to Norman times, though nothing remains of the original building. When the 14th century church in Decorated style was built, some traces of the earlier Norman building were discovered, including window arches with dogtooth ornamentation. When this church replaced the Norman building, it stood the test of time, and served as parish church to the folk of Braunston for nearly 500 years.

Although there was a substantial amount of material from the previous church, it was not enough to ensure the complete construction of the new building. The contrast in colours in the tower comes from the use of Duston stone, with its delightful golden-brown colour and which was used for the base, and the old dark red sandstone from the previous church. Weldon stone, with its contrasting but distinctive silver-grey appearance, was used for both the spire and the tracery.

All Saint's majestic, tapering, unforgettable 150 foot (65 metre) high spire dominates the surrounding countryside, making it conspicuous from many directions. Prominently situated on higher ground at the A45 end of the village's long High Street, this elegant, even noble, crocketted spire standing atop the tower is an unmistakable landmark. The west tower, created in Decorated style, holds the spire aloft: at the base of this there is an ornamental parapet, and from the tower's four corners superbly crafted pinnacles arise.

A cursory glance does little to identify the beauty of this feature of the building, and more time is needed to take in its structure, style and appeal. It has three tiers of lucarnes – small openings to allow light to enter – and the rich decoration includes many crockets – floral carvings. Although attractive from ground level, the stonemason's art must be even more appealing close up.

There is an interesting tale which suggests that the bells from the church at Willoughby – just over the county border in Warwickshire – and less than two miles as the crow flies, were also taken to the same bellfoundry at the same time as Braunston's were being recast. If the story is true, Willoughby now has the tenor bell that belonged to Braunston, and Willoughby's bell is said to grace the tower at Braunston.

There is a ring of six musical bells, all of which were cast in 1811. In 1552 the church had four bells, together with a sanctus bell. Just over a hundred years later in 1672, these already ancient bells were taken to the bellfoundry of Richard Jones in Woodstock, where they were cast into a ring of six. In the 19th century these same bells were once again removed from the tower and taken to Hereford to be recast before they were rehung in 1811. As with many bells, their weight in the tower caused a problem, and a new steel frame was provided for them towards the end of the 1920, ensuring that they could be rung without fear of causing damage to the main structure of the church.

The church clock was the work of John Hanbury of West Haddon and was made in 1824. It was removed from the badly damaged earlier tower, and reinstalled in the new one.

The inspiring nature of the church's exterior is carried on into the building, where the impression of a spacious interior is confirmed when entering through the south door. Here, at least in summer, on either side of the porch there are tubs of welcoming flowers. The relatively long nave with its five bays has somewhat uninspiring chamfered arches. Supported by octagonal pillars there is a clerestory – the upper part of the nave wall that has windows – above them. It is these high windows, with their clear glass, which help flood the church with light.

The Church of St Mary has both north and south aisles. In attempting to put the building into proportion, Hussey was responsible for widening the body of the church, vitally important for an expanding congregation. The heights of the various roofs were also raised, again in an effort to produce a better proportioned building. It was also said this was done to ensure that the outstanding tower should not detract from the worship area. However, in spite of these changes, many people would probably still argue that the tower remains a particularly striking feature!

Although many changes were made to the original church during its rebuilding, some historical features were retained. By far the oldest is several superb arches, including the Perpendicular tower arch, the narrow easterly arch in the south chapel and, also from the Perpendicular period, the chancel arches. Though the latter retains some of its original work, it was 'improved' in Victorian times when a very large chamfer was added.

When the Rev Clough moved on, the new incumbent was not entirely happy with the interior of he building, and the architect William Butterfield was brought in to carry out some further restoration in 1874. An architect of some note, he was responsible for the designs of a number of buildings, including the school buildings in nearby Rugby, together with the chapel at Oxford's Balliol College and several colonial cathedrals.

Butterfield's work included the commissioning of a new font, fashioned from pink marble, which stands at the west end of the central aisle. A closer investigation shows it has elaborate carvings with ornate designs. Perhaps not surprisingly the water jug standing at the base of the font is enhanced by intricate designs that have been inspired by canalware ornamentation, and which have been carried out with meticulous care.

Other restoration work by Butterfield included the north windows, which he redesigned, and H. Hughes was responsible for the design of the stained glass in these. Attractive as they are, it is perhaps Butterfield's rather ornate stone reredos, bearing the inscription *Sanctus, sanctus, sanctus*, which once attracted the eye. However, Butterfield's bold designs were obviously not always appreciated by later churchgoers, and his reredos was covered with an oak one in 1928. To accommodate this, the east window was raised. Above this was a painted cross, but it is no longer visible. Stained glass windows were also put in, and though these are an attractive feature, they have cut out some of the light in the chancel. Butterfield was also responsible for the changes to the timber roof supports, which he covered with brown and silver painted roof boards.

There is a modern altar in the south chapel bearing a dedication to St. Giles, to whom the original building was dedicated. There are several stained glass windows, one of the most striking being in the centre of the south chapel, and ascribed to William Wailes (1849). The east window is a memorial to the Rev. A. B. Clough (as mentioned earlier, he was the instigator of the 1800s rebuilding). The nave also contains an interesting lectern and reading desk, both of which were carved by Trevor Cox in 1956. The lectern has a number of Celtic figures representing the four evangelists, the design having been copied from the Book of Kells. The High Victorian church furniture in the nave are good examples of its type, and shows the excellent craft of the woodworker.

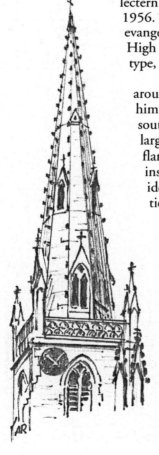

Cross-legged knights seem to feature in several churches in and around Daventry, and Braunston is no exception. Pevsner referred to him as "excessively cross-legged"! This particular knight is in the south chancel, and is mid-14th century in origin. The figure has a large shield by his side, with a pillow supporting his head, angels flanking him and his feet placed on two strange beasts. Careful inspection shows that they are standing on a man of the cloth. The identity of this knight can be deduced from the rose emblem positioned between his feet. This is of the de Ros family, and from the style of the armour, historians suggest that it may be a memorial to William 4th Baron Ros, who died in 1352 while on a pilgrimage to the Holy Land. He is shielded by a gabled canopy.

The head of a former, much damaged, large churchyard cross is kept in the north-west corner of the church and close to the Norman altar. This would have been in the churchyard at one time, and is thought to be 14th century in origin. It has scenes from the Crucifixion, a priest with robes, the Virgin Mary and Jesus, and an armed soldier. A later stone, bearing the initials R.B. and the date 1672, stands close by. It is thought that this might have been carved to record work to the steeple – at the time the Rector was Richard Burden, probably solving the R.B. mystery! Like most churches, All Saints boasts a long line of rectors, beginning in the 1200s. Over the centuries there must have been some illustrious characters that occupied the tenancy. One of these was Edward Reynolds, who was a member of what was known as the Presbyterian Party. This group was involved in a variety of clerical controversies during the Civil War. In spite of what might be considered misde-meanours, Reynolds went on to become Bishop of Norwich. Although not generally known, he also made a name for himself in religious his-tory, because he was responsible for writing the General Thanksgiving in the *Book of Common Prayer.*

In spite of the arrival of a new font, the previous font, dating back to Norman times, still remains as a feature of the church, and rests in he north aisle. In comparison to its modern counterpart it is less ornate, and shows its age after some 900 or so years, with its worn – or maybe even vandalised – carved rope mouldings near the top.

Another relic from an earlier church is the piscina in the vestry. It has been suggested that it is likely this would originally have been positioned close to one of the altars in one of the side chapels.

The church also possesses a complete set of registers, the first entry of which was made in 1538. During the rebuilding, some historical monu-ments obviously vanished, including a tombstone for Gregory Isham.

brockhall
church of st peter and st paul

Although a number of the churches in the Daventry area are conspicuous, there are others that are almost secretively hidden away. Such is the case with the Church of St Peter and St Paul at Brockhall. A narrow road takes you from either Flore on the A45, or the A5 (north of Weedon), with the last part of the journey through parkland that has been a feature for hundreds of year. Opposite the church, thatched cottages add to the charm and tranquillity of the small settlement, with its 10 households and a population of 20 where – in spite of modernisation to properties and 20th century paraphernalia – time seems almost to have stood still. Somehow, not even the continuous sound of M1 traffic not that far distant can destroy the atmosphere.

The path leading to the church is overshadowed by tall yew trees, and on the walk through the churchyard there is a constant reminder of the past. The many ancient burial sites – including a number of very old table tombs, their inscriptions long lost to the wind and rain – reinforces the fact that this is a community which has thrived for centuries.

The foundations of the present church can be traced back to about 1200. The building which was begun in Norman times was completed over the centuries, with later major work taking place in the Perpendicular style. Two types of stone have been used: the harder limestone contrasts sharply with the softer brown stone, with its bands of iron. A glance at various areas of external fabric shows how this softer stone has eroded much more significantly than the harder, lighter limestone. A variety of lichens have established themselves on part of the stonework, showing that even in these polluted times, the air around Brockhall remains relatively clean.

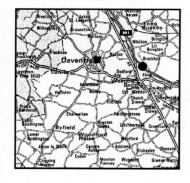

The neat west tower of this building, almost overshadowed by the Hall, is at least a century later than the earliest parts of the church, and was erected in the 14th or early 15th centuries. It has a lancet window on its west face, and additional battlements were added after the original building work had been completed. The tower's west wall is thicker in the middle, and the reinforcement was probably put in place to take the weight of a bell cote. During its construction, the tower was built into the fabric of the church. There are three bells in the tower, the oldest of which bears no inscription and is purportedly from 1300. A second bell, now cracked, was made by Newcome of Leicester in 1609, and the third and final bell, a Priest's bell, was cast in 1820.

The whole of the outside north wall, including the plinth and buttresses, have been dated at about 1400. Entrance is through the 15th century south porch, which has leaded windows containing clear glass, and which shelters the earlier 13th century south door, with its moulded arch. Some speculation has arisen as to the original design of the church, one theory being that the nave was probably arranged as two squares, which would explain why much of the outer south wall of the nave is relatively thin when compared to the outside walls of most other churches. Today, the church of St Peter and St Paul consists of a chancel, nave, south aisle, west tower, north-west vestry and a south porch.

Before the tower was constructed, various parts of the church were already in place, owing their existence to the work of 13th century craftsmen at least a hundred years before the tower rose from the same site. These earlier works include the superbly executed south doorway, and three bays found in the south arcade. The window in the south aisle is square-headed and of the Perpendicular period, made of two lancets which are under the one hood mould. The east window was replaced in the 19th century.

At the same time as the tower was being built, work also took place inside the church, when the nave was given a new west bay, and another bay was also added so that it embraced the bell tower, which was built onto the west wall. The south aisle was also widened and elongated so that it could take in the now enlarged nave. The arch that separates the main body of the church from the tower is of a three-chamfered design.

There is some debate about the south aisle. It is possible that it may be of the same date as the south arcade, or it could be that the original

Although two of the slightly chamfered south arcade arches are round, and held on circular piers, with their simple square moulded capitals, and square abaci (the flat slab on top of the capital), the newer arch at the western-most end has a two-centred arch with polygonal responds (a half pier which is incorporated into a wall, and carries one end of an arch).

arch was made wider in the 13th century. The north wall has two two-light windows that date from about 1400, and contain tracery and quatrefoils. The north doorway, also dating from the same time, features two chamfered orders, of which the outer one is sunk. The vestry was formed when the west part of the south aisle was filled in the 19th century. The window in this part of the building has a single light, with its trefoil head.

Because of the relatively small size of the interior of the church, the north respond of the chancel arch has been set back and is in the angle between the nave and the chancel. This has resulted in a greater span for the chancel arch than would otherwise have been possible. The chancel is now shorter than it was in earlier centuries, and this later work was carried out under the direction of the architect E. F. Law in the 19th century. He was also responsible for restoration work on a number of other churches in Northamptonshire. As with most churches, alterations and restoration work has taken place over the centuries. The surrounds to the south and north doorways have been altered, and are much more modern. Of Gothic appearance, they originate from 1830–40. Although the nave is from the Romanesque period, the roof is only from 1874, and from the same period that the chancel was altered.

The piscina, with its trefoil head and rounded foils, is positioned at the east end of the south wall, where there would have been an altar at one time when this part of the church was used as a chapel. In the south aisle, to the west of the piscina, is a large tomb recess that dates from around 1340. It is complete with a substantial cusped arch, beneath which is a second arch with a trefoil shape. The copious ornamentation includes a wealth of ballflower decorations and crockets, the result of the early 13th century craftsman's skill. The top pinnacles were probably added in the 19th century.

The east window, of the Perpendicular period, consists of three lights which have cinquefoil heads to the lights and pierced spandrels. A spandrel is the almost triangular space between one side of the outer curve of an arch. This is in contrast to the south window that has two lancets. The east window, with its figures of Jesus, the saints and angels, was erected to perpetuate the memory of the Rev. Philip Thornton, who was Rector of Brockhall from 1806 to 1869, and was put in at the time of the 1874 restoration work. The church's most historic glass dates from the late 14th century, and consists of two small roundels situated in the north window of the nave. Most other windows are plain, although some of them have a variety of motifs, and especially in the trefoils on the north wall. The octagonal font is from the Perpendicular period, and fleurons (rosette decorations) have been carved at the base of the bowl.

One family in particular is remembered by a variety of memorial tablets. The well-known Thornton family has been compared to the Knightleys of Fawsley as having a great deal of influence in the county. John Thornton bought the Hall from Lawrence Eyton in 1625. However, unlike memorials to the Knightley family in St Mary's Church at Fawsley and All Saints Church, Norton, most of those for the Thorntons are fairly plain, although some of the earlier ones bear more ornamentation. The first of these memorials was erected sometime in the early 1700s; the last in the late 1800s. The tablet to Thomas Thornton is the work of William Cox, and is dated 1783.

Hatchments which are on display on the south aisle arches are to members of the Thornton family, and were originally executed between about 1790 and 1862. As with hatchments in other churches, they were used as part of the funeral procession and mourning period, before being returned to the church where they were hung.

An attractive modern feature of the church is the altar frontal. Produced by Mrs G. Myles in 1982, it represents peace, and was produced at the time of the Falklands War. The colours have been chosen carefully, and the greys and mauves were used to represent the sadness of the tragic event. The frontal includes a large P for Pax (peace). This modern piece of craftsmanship is in contrast to that of the older, more solid, nature of the stones, and it hangs on the altar for all to see.

byfield
church of the holy cross

The ancient village of Byfield has been occupied at least since Saxon times. The name comes from two Saxon words which mean 'a habitation' (bye) and a 'field' (fielde), and was first used for the settlement to distinguish it from what would, at the time it was established, have been nothing more than wasteland outside the parameters of the place to be called Byfield. It goes without saying that the area has changed many times since it first appeared. The *Domesday Book* provides some interesting information – when it was written (1086) Byfield had four separate Manors, with associated buildings.

At the beginning of a new Millennium the church still stands as a living testimony to the Christian faith that has been a feature of the area for centuries. Historians speculate that a church has been a hallmark of the village for at least nine hundred years. It is possible that, like many other settlements, earlier buildings made available for Christian worship also sprang up in this village. The present church's history goes back to at least 1340, confirmed by its architectural style going back more than 650 years.

Historians believe that there was an earlier church on the site which had its origins around 1242. There are some who suggest that the earlier building might never have been completed. Again, speculation, supported by some evidence, reveals that even this early church was not the first religious building in the settlement, as one Robert de Rothelent – who was ensconced as a sub-tenant of Hugh, Earl of Chester – is known to have handed over the church of "Bivivella in Northamptonescire" (original spelling) to the Abbey of Ebrulf, at Utica in Normandy (France). This was at some point during the reign of the first William, and the King confirmed the grant in 1081. The Normandy link came about through Hugh Grentemaisnill, a Norman baron who came to England with William the Conqueror and was probably involved at the Battle of Hastings.

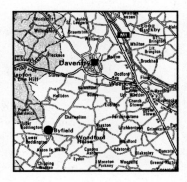

The first written reference to a church in Byfield is in 1291, when the earlier church was *in situ*. At this time a woman called Agnes went into Holy Cross church to seek sanctuary for fear of being arrested. It is interesting to note that the church had already changed its dedication from Helena to All Saints. According to accounts from the time, Agnes admitted to her crimes, and "confessed divers thefts and abjured (renounced on oath) the realm".

Many changes occurred over the centuries, until eventually Sir Richard Knightley of Fawsley, some four or five miles from Byfield, acquired the patronage, probably paying a great deal of money for it. Thus began, as in several other places, a long tradition of association between Fawsley, the Knightley family and a particular village – in this case Byfield. The name Knightley appears not infrequently in the list of Rectors over the succeeding centuries. The Knightleys held the patronage until 1820, when the President and Fellows of Corpus Christi College, Oxford acquired it. They are still the Patrons of the living of Byfield.

Today's church stands close to a thatched cottage, which somehow adds to the timelessness. The building was originally dedicated to St Helena or St Helen, the mother of the Roman Emperor Constantine, who was the first Roman Emperor to become a Christian. According to the legend, Constantine's mother, who was also a Christian, went to the Holy Land where it is said she discovered the cross on which Jesus had been crucified. It was because of this that a number of churches in England – including that at Byfield – were dedicated to her. However, the church is now dedicated to the Holy Cross, because all churches dedicated to Helena were re-dedicated when it was discovered that Helena was not of English nationality.

The church that stands today, with its substantial tall tower, is clearly visible from the A361 when approaching from the Banbury direction. It stands in the ancient village which straddles the A361, and which today is relatively large, with a population of around 1200. Like so many other churches around Daventry, Byfield's building is doubly conspicuous because of its spire and its position, perched on a raised knoll.

Battlements, and a pinnacle at each corner, enhance the tower, which is crowned with a later small recessed – but nonetheless distinctive – spire, and this exhibits two tiers of lucarnes arranged in alternating directions. There are five stages to the tower, and one of the characteristics of this particular period is that the architects and builders

ABJURATION

In the 13th century, the church was the only place where criminals could seek refuge from arrest, and they were allowed to stay there for a maximum of forty days. The criminal could ask for a coroner to be called, and the offender would take an oath of abjuration, in which the individual agreed to leave the country. Having done this, the person would be released from 'custody'. However, the individual was not free, and had to make his or her own way to a seaport, the destination already decided by the coroner.

used vertical lines of intersecting ribwork – tracery. It is the height of the tower (120 feet (37 m)) that makes it such a distinctive feature of the landscape. The upper part of the tower reflects the Perpendicular period, and there are two superb widely spaced bell openings linked by an arch, called 'basket type'. In this, the lintel joining the two openings is connected to the jambs using concave 90° curves.

In spite of the ancient nature of the church, the ring of eight bells in the tower is relatively modern, with four dating from 1703, a fifth from 1791, and the treble cast in Birmingham in 1905. The two most recent bells were placed in the tower in 1991. There is also a chiming clock in the tower, installed in commemoration of Queen Victoria's Diamond Jubilee. At the same time, the existing six bells were also rehung. In 1947, new fittings had been made for the bells, when the frame was overhauled and the bells rehung.

An attractive west doorway with a splendid portal also enhances the tower. This doorway is worth a closer look, because the 14th century carvings are particularly handsome. The surrounds retain some of the craftsmanship of earlier stonemasons, and the continuous line of ball flowers are particularly attractive – though some are less distinctive than when they first appeared, having suffered from the elements. There are also pinnacles, together with a crocketted (carvings of leaf shapes) ogee (a semicircular arch with a pronounced 'point') hood mould over the top of the door. The window above the niches has nodding ogee arches on both the left and right, and there is also a third niche above it.

As you approach the church along its well-kept paths, the ancient trees guard and protect it. Now pause for a while and reflect on the building of this superb and important place of Christian worship. The 14th century church in Decorated style was built from local ironstone, probably extracted from the fields to the south of the village, where a number of depressions remain. Imagine, too, the local people bringing it using simple equipment, and then the skilled craftsmen fashioning the stone bit by bit to form the building we see today.

Over the ensuing centuries, a range of restorative and renovative activities have taken place. From about the time that Holy Cross was being built, buildings were becoming more ornate, after the rather simple and plain architecture of earlier building styles.

The Church of the Holy Cross was completed a few years before the arrival of the Black Death that was the forerunner of a new outbreak of virulent disease. Whilst it was rife, this epidemic decimated the population of villages like Byfield, and it was especially prevalent in amongst the inhabitants between May and October 1349.

Entrance is through the extremely large south porch, of similar design to the west one, and with small two-light windows in the side. It is worth pausing here for a few moments to take in the ancient Byfield bier which was restored by the parishioners in 1987, and which is now on view for all to see. During routine inspection work it was discovered that the gargoyles – which had been a feature of the tower for a many centuries – were in a dangerous state. These were removed, and have found a resting place here to be viewed by all and sundry! Undoubtedly described as unattractive – even ugly – these carvings originally occupied positions on the nave roof.

Once through the south door, the interior of this mainly Decorated village church gives a feeling of space and freedom. One problem that is common to most PCCs is the deterioration in the building material. Built from the attractively coloured local stone, with its relatively soft texture, it is prone to erosion, and this advances the longer the church stands. It particularly accelerated in the 18th century with the arrival of the Industrial Revolution. In 1870, an architect suggested that not only was the roof in a precarious state, but problems with the rest of the building posed a danger to local people. Taking this report to heart, considerable rebuilding work took place, and in addition to re-roofing the building, much of the church was rebuilt. At this time, the restorers also took the opportunity to renew the nave roof, returning it to its original pitch.

> At one time the monks from Trafford House, not far from Culworth, occupied the church porch, together with the south aisle and the south chapel. They attended Sunday service in Byfield, and regularly occupied a part of the church that came to be known as the 'Trafford' (south) aisle. Having commuted from Trafford House for Sunday worship, the monks would then spend the rest of the day in the porch, resting and refreshing themselves, ready to take part in evensong.

During the restoration work the stone crosses, now displayed on the north wall of the nave, were discovered. It is believed they date from the 13th century. It was also decided to increase the length of the north aisle so that a proper organ could be accommodated to replace the barrel organ. In spite of this restoration work, further deterioration of the external fabric continued, and fifty years ago it became necessary to take further action. The outline of the tower was changed when four octagonal turrets, one at each corner, were removed. Weathering has also removed a number of pencil sundials that were a feature of the outside walls. It is possible to see faint traces of one of these close to the south porch door.

By far the most striking feature of the church interior is the chancel, with its tall, slender decorated two-light windows. Many of the nave windows, together with the east one, came under the scrutiny of the 19th century Victorian restorers, and several owe their existence to Kempe, including the small west windows in the tower (1893), the east window (1897), with the large south window in the chancel receiving his attention in the early 20th century (1902). The east window shows Palm Sunday to the Deposition, and above these Biblical illustrations is a pelican, the symbol of piety, as well as being the emblem of Corpus Christi College.

It is also thought that Kempe may also have been responsible for the window at the south aisle's east end. Kempe's influence can also be seen in at least one other window, where an employee by the name of Towers produced the western window in the north aisle. Whitefriars installed that to the east, known as the Easter Window. (It is possible to identify the makers of the glass from their marks that appear in the bottom of the windows.)

The two north aisle windows show the empty tomb after the Resurrection, and the presentation of Jesus in the temple. Other windows with glass worth more than a casual glance include that in the Trafford Aisle (south transept), which is of St. Anne, St. Thomas and St. George, all patron saints of the Fairbrother family, whose burials took place in the churchyard in close proximity to the exterior wall of the aisle. This window is also attributed to Kempe. A further window in the Trafford Aisle shows Christ at his Crucifixion on the Cross, with the Virgin Mary and St. John, one on either side.

> *The low window in the south chancel is possibly the long lost Leper Window. This was once again revealed in the chancel when restoration work was carried out in 1870. The idea was that lepers could stand outside the church but see the elevation of the host.*

Very little medieval stained glass was left in the windows, and what remained was salvaged and is now in safe keeping. The two medieval stained glass roundels which were removed from Byfield Church are on loan to Ely Stained Glass Museum, where they are on view during the Museum's open season (Easter to the end of October). This stained glass is 15th century in origin, and one roundel shows a hind (deer) sitting on grass and flower-covered mound.

Internal furniture has also seen some changes at Byfield. In the 1960s the high altar was taken from its traditional position and placed on a plinth in the chancel. In 1990 it was decided to have a new nave altar, and at the same time a decision was taken to return the original one to its former site. The nave, with its four bays of double chamfered arches in Decorated style, contains a number of very old benches, some of which show intricate traceried panels on the backs, sides and front. The nave houses two pulpits: one is a tall Georgian affair, which is still in use; the other is from the Victorian era, and is now redundant.

Some ancient tombs rest against the west wall in the graveyard, and these include a number of extremely old coffins which were discovered when the 1879 restoration work was taking place.

canon's ashby
priory church of st mary

The present Priory Church of St Mary's represents a mere fragment of what was at one time a large Augustinian Priory. Founded in Henry II's reign between 1153 and 1189, it was Stephen de Lisye, Lord of the Manor, who was responsible for its appearance. To ensure that the institution would be self-sufficient, various endowments were made, which included an amount of land, houses, a croft, a mill and fishponds. The original building must have been an elaborate affair, based on the traditional priory plan. However, the building never possessed a south aisle, and the cloister would unusually have joined directly onto the nave.

Today, the present church consists of two bays of what was at one time a much longer five-bay nave and north aisle, together with a substantial north-west tower. The total length of the original building would probably have been almost 220 feet (66m), some four times the length of the present structure. The current building is extremely large, with two tall two-light bell openings in Decorated style. The tower was constructed much later than the initial foundation, and was added to the north of the aisle in the mid-14th century. It also has battlements, together with four large and distinctive pinnacles. Buttresses on the east wall of the tower help to take the strain of its extra weight.

The tower, originally contained a ring of six bells, but was unable to support the massive weight, so they were removed and sold, though a single bell was left bearing an inscription, which when translated means "Blessed be the Name of the Lord". In his *History of Northamptonshire,* Bridges tells us that in the early 1760s the last bell had found a resting place in the corner of the church. There is some speculation that two of the bells from Canon's Ashby Church found their way to nearby Blakesley Church, where they hang in the tower.

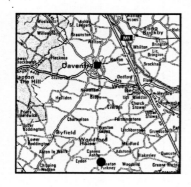

The superb portal at the west front of the nave is thought to date from about 1250, although the Perpendicular window that towers above it came later.

Exhibiting some marvellous contrasts in colour, with dark ironstone columns and white ashlar arches, the ornamentation is superb. The portal is complete with shafts, and includes an elaborate arch with a number of fine mouldings. Stiff leaf capitals enhance the elegance of this range of moulded arches. This west front, with its origins way back between 1230 and 1240, still retains the original doorway – where more than 700 years later the woodcarver's skill remains visible. Above the doorway a large Perpendicular window has five spacious lights, with well executed shafts enhanced with stiff leaf carvings on the capitals (tops of the columns), and rounded off with a lavishly moulded arch. There are 13th century bays on either side with blank arcading and rounded quatrefoils, above which are superbly moulded arches.

Entrance to the church is through a side gate, the path leading through the magnificent west door. Once inside, it is the aura of what remains of this impressive building which takes a few moments to sink in. The nave is especially high, and tall piers support the south aisle, with its two bays of soaring arches, complete with triple chamfers.

Various windows are of post-Reformation origin, thought to date from the late Jacobean period, including those in the south wall of the nave and the east window. The latter has glass showing a scene from the Nativity; to the north of this are portrayed the figures of St. Augustine and the Prophet Isaiah; and to the south can be seen images of St. Luke and St. Bernard. The glass in this window was added in the memory of Mary Dryden, a member of the well-known Dryden family which occupied nearby Canon's Ashby House, who died in 1916. A painted frieze enhances the window. The glass in the south wall consists of plain material. Still in the nave, there is an octagonal font, the bowl of which has a range of decorations carved on it, not dissimilar to those used in window tracery.

Not surprisingly a number of memorials to the Dryden family have been placed in the church over the centuries, the oldest of which is in

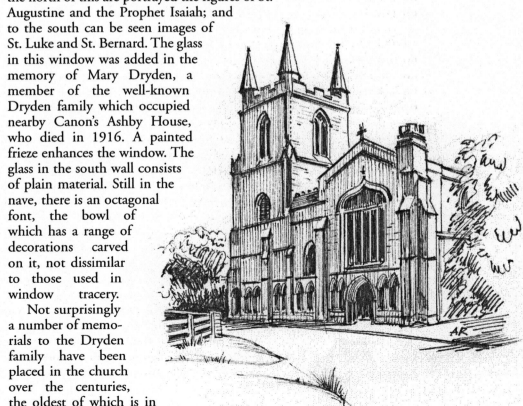

the floor of the nave. It is a brass to John Dryden, who died in 1584, and takes the form of a 23 in (57 cm) figure standing be-robed and with his hands in prayer, above his head the family crest.

There are other memorials to this noble family, including that on the north wall of the sanctuary, which is undoubtedly the most striking. This is in memory of John Turner Dryden who died in 1757. In this particular Dryden monument, the sculptor has incorporated an urn, with a large female figure seated beside it. It also incorporates the family coat of arms. It is worth pausing to read the wording on the stone.

> *The work of the sculptor John Rossi, this memorial was added some years later since Rossi began his studies at the Royal Academy in 1781. He was also sculptor to the Prince Regent and William IV, and was responsible for many monuments in London's St Paul's Cathedral.*

> *On some fond breast the parting Soul relies;*
> *Some pious drops the closing Eye requires;*
> *Even from the Tomb the voice of nature cries.*
> *Even in our ashes live their wonted fires.*

A monument of a similar, though somewhat simpler, design to John Edward Turner Dryden, Baronet, who died in 1818, stands opposite on the south wall. Produced by the same sculptor, the monument features a Grecian woman in mourning holding a garland in her hand that she is about to lay on an altar.

The Dryden family crest can be found in the nave, above the tomb of Sir Robert Dryden, who died in 1708. Two brasses also in the nave, at the east end, are to John Dryden (1631) and Erasmus (1662), and Dame Frances (1630). Set into the wall of the same part of the church's aisle are heraldic brasses in memory of Sir Erasmus, Alfred Dryden and Sir Arthur Dryden, Tenth Baronet. Erasmus, born in 1821, died in 1912. His wife is also remembered. Sir Arthur passed away in 1938. The plaques on the east wall of the north aisle are in memory of two of the Dryden family who died fighting for their country. Captain Wilfred Dryden Pritchard, of the Royal Field Artillery, who was killed in action near Neuve Chapelle on or about 25 September 1915, and Lawrence Dryden Pritchard of the Fifth London Regiment was 28 when he died on 28 August 1918 in action in Hendicourt. Other memorials here include those to Muriel Dryden and her husband Cecil. At the time of their deaths he was 66 and she was 81.

A Gothic architectural tablet recording the death of the Rev. Sir Henry Dryden (1837) and his wife Elizabeth (1851) is on the east wall in the north aisle. Further memorials here are to Alfred Curwen Dryden (1938), Louisa Isabella Pritchard (1948), Cecil Dryden (1959), Muriel Dryden (1978) and John Lawrence and Mary Katharine Dryden, 1982 and 1997, respectively.

According to Kitchin (*Hatchments of Britain – Northamptonshire, Warwickshire and Worcestershire*), eleven hatchments to the Drydens have been preserved in Canon's Ashby. They are still on view in various places in the church, some almost too high to view comfortably. These adornments, bearing the family coat of arms, would have taken pride of place at Dryden family funerals. After the mourning period at the house, they would have been returned to the church. In addition, there are some other interesting artefacts that remind us of the life of Sir Robert Dryden, who died in 1708. This display includes some of his armour, which can be seen on the south wall of the nave. Made up of a number of pieces, it includes two pennons, helmet and crest, wreath, tabard, shield, a pair of gauntlets and spurs, together with a sword and banners.

The Decorated tower doorway in the south still has its medieval oak door. A tablet on the west wall to the south of the door is to Gervase Jackson-Stops, Architectural Adviser to the National Trust ,"who loved this place".

Outside in the churchyard there is a ubiquitous yew, leaning at an interesting angle, and this antiquary keeps company with many of the headstones, a number of which have almost sunk without trace, as they have dipped into the Northamptonshire soil. But undeniably the most striking feature is a replica of a Celtic cross. This was erected in memory of Sir Henry Dryden, who died in 1899. This particular design is used because it was one that he discovered and had drawn in the Orkneys. Today it still stands proudly in his memory.

Although steeped in more than 800 years of history, the church is still used regularly for worship, including short services on Sunday afternoons. For more information, check the noticeboard by the church gate.

charwelton
church of the holy trinity

The village street from Charwelton leads along a gated road to the site of a settlement that is now no more. Aptly named 'Church Charwelton', there is little which remains of the earlier community, the religious house being the most substantial structure left. Today the building stands nearly isolated amidst delightful rolling Northamptonshire countryside, with nothing more than the farm animals, residents of Church Farm, and the occupants of a nearby cottage for company. Travelling either along the metalled gated road or the more rural Jurassic Way footpath, the church tower seems to be playing a game of hide and seek (a kind of now you see me, now you don't) as it cautiously peeps out from behind the ancient trees which keep it company in this relatively isolated part of Northamptonshire.

It is fascinating to speculate as to why the earlier village of Charwelton disappeared. Over the centuries many hypotheses and counter-theories have been put forward, and vigorously debated. A look back to the 14th century may provide some explanation. During this period the now extinct village covered the area around the church. When the Daventry to Banbury road was re-aligned, a packhorse bridge was also constructed. The original village has been listed as a 'safe inn', and such places relied very much on both an easy access and a quick getaway. With the change in the route of the road, the area where the church stood was less accessible, and for obvious reasons, people preferred to be closer to the new road.

Historians also suggest that during the War of the Roses, the village was infiltrated by soldiers billeted in Daventry. During their visits they caused considerable damage to the former village – another reason for moving to new, and hopefully safer, surroundings. The new village is some three-quarters of a mile distant from the deserted settlement and church. At the historic site of Church Charwelton, you can see many mounds and hollows in the surrounding fields which give an indication of the site and extent of the former village. Although these are fairly easy to detect, they are even more significant when viewed on an aerial photograph of the now depopulated village. If further evidence is needed of an earlier settlement, this is provided by the remains of fishponds and associated earthworks in the immediate area.

The medieval church, dedicated to the Holy Trinity, was once the property of the ancient priory of Bittlesden in Buckinghamshire. The 13th century south doorway leads into a porch with a stone-vaulted roof. There is an outer stairway, which leads to what was probably in earlier times a priest's room. One of the features of Holy Trinity which has mystified historians for some time is the 'scratch dial' on the outer wall of the south chapel. At first sight it appears to bear the date 1171, with all the rays carved on the right-hand side of the dial. What is puzzling is whether the dial's date is genuine or faked. The reason for such misgivings about its authenticity is that, as far as historians are aware, at this time figures like 1171 were always written as Roman numerals. The question is — if the dial's date is genuine, is this the earliest record of Arabian numerals? It seems likely that the query will never be answered, and the exact date at which the scratch dial was produced will remain a mystery.

The tower, a striking and memorable edifice, is quite large, and owes its existence to the skills of our 13th and 14th century mason ancestors, who erected it between 1290 and 1350. Built in the Decorated style, it features four well-executed bell openings, and buttresses support, and battlements adorn, the structure. The west window is plain, but a closer inspection of the west doorway shows the remains of what are bellflower decorations. There are also figures staring out at onlooker, as they have done for hundreds of years. "In 1552 there were iij bells in ye steeple and a sanct bell" — today the church possesses a peal of four bells, the heaviest of which is the tenor and weighs some 11cwt (approx. 560kg), and two of which, the treble and number 2, were recast by John Taylor & Son of Loughborough in 1847. Further work also took place at the turn of the 20th century

The path takes the visitor along the same route that the Jurassic Way walkers use, but a diversion to the right,

ensures you make it to the south porch. Inside, the large tower arch is also of the same period as the tower. Worth searching for are two corbels depicting men's heads – who has been portrayed thus will never be known, but it is fascinating to speculate that they could either be the craftsmen who fashioned them or maybe local dignitaries – such as the squire.

The clerestoried nave in the north arcade is resplendent and enhanced by three arcades on either side. Piers hold the slender arches aloft, as they have since they were first carved in the early 14th century. Here medieval artists practised their skills by carving a range of stone heads. In contrast, the lower arches found in the south arcade have octagonal piers, and their double chamfered arches are probably slightly earlier; possibly from the beginning of the previous century. Standing in the north aisle is a medieval font, carved with rich decoration, showing roses, oak leaves and emblems of the Holy Trinity, and produced during the reign of Elizabeth I.

For many hundreds of years the church was the resting places of the locally dominant Andrewes family. As with the Knightleys at nearby Fawsley, they were well-known and profitable sheep farmers. Of the monuments, the three fine brasses are worthy of closer inspection. Their varying styles of dress show progressive changes through the centuries. The oldest memorial is to the 15th century landowner Thomas Andrewes, who died in 1496. Included on the brass is his wife Margaret, with both wearing ermine gowns, though Margaret is further adorned with an elaborate head dress. Their eight children share the canopy. The adult figures are depicted as 4ft tall (120cm) impressions. During the next generation of the Andrewes family, marriage resulted in a linking of this well-known local family with the equally important Knightley family, when a son – also called Thomas – married Emme. The third of the Thomas's died in 1541, and his wife Agnes accompanies him on his brass. She can be seen wearing a large headdress, and a gown with long hanging sleeves, the fashion of the day – different from that on earlier brasses. Thomas has no covering for his head, but wears a suit of armour.

Emme died in 1490; her husband in about 1530. On her 3 ft (90cm) brass tomb she too wears a very richly decorated dress reminiscent of her standing, and which bestows upon her engraving the necessary air of rich opulence. Thomas presents a regal figure dressed in a tournament suit of armour. There is further armour behind his head, together with the customary animal at his feet; in this case a dog. Their seven children are also shown on the tomb, and are arranged in two groups – four sons and three daughters. These are called 'weepers'.

If you cast your eyes beyond the font onto the west wall of the south aisle, you will see the memorial to Sir Thomas Andrewes, who died in 1564. It takes the form of a free-standing alabaster tomb chest. Closer examination shows that Thomas was twice married; both of his wives are shown on the memorial, with the carvings of the three recumbent figures having been well executed. The tomb also incorporates a variety of shields, some of which take the form of roundels. The tomb also reveals that Thomas had a total of twelve children, all of whom are included on the memorial. In addition there are two babies in cradles.

daventry
holy cross

The impressive obelisk spire of Holy Cross, crowned with a cross – and floodlit during the darker months of the year – is a landmark as the town is approached, almost peeping from the growing trees which may eventually swamp it and reduce the view. Situated just off the market square in the ancient town, Holy Cross has the distinction of being the only Northamptonshire town church erected in the 18th century. The present church is much as it was when it was completed, with few alterations being made since the original construction. However, a central porch was added which, although created two hundred years later in 1951, is in the same style as the rest of the building.

Although the history of the present Parish Church of the Holy Cross is relatively recent compared with many other churches in the area, nevertheless it has a pedigree that goes back many centuries. Historians are willing to admit that they cannot pinpoint the date at which Christianity arrived in the town, but it is known that the site on which Holy Cross stands has been 'praising the Lord' for nigh on a thousand years. Historic records show that at the time of the Norman Conquest, there was a church in Daventry, and although it is believed that this was the first church, it is possible that some kind of building was in existence some time prior to the Norman invasion. As Saxon churches were of wooden construction, they were unlikely to survive the ravages of the elements. Records of the earlier church are sketchy, and information is difficult to access, so certain suppositions have to be made. One such is that perhaps part of the Saxon building – much changed, layered and ravaged by at least two fires – had been incorporated into the various changes which took place over the centuries.

The church in Daventry would have been a place from which missionaries went out to other villages to preach and minister. It is known that Hugh de Leicester, who founded a Cluniac Monastery at Preston Capes some five miles to the south of Daventry, was unhappy with the siting of the building close to the castle. It is said that he was also concerned because there was a lack of water in Preston Capes. With these excuses the monks made the move to Daventry, and when they arrived they took over the church. Whether they sought approval for their move is not known, but it was more than sixty years until the Archbishop of Canterbury approved the take over.

In addition to having the church, the monks also erected a priory to the honour St. Mary of La Charite and St Augustine, on a site close to the present church. Before the establishment of the new priory, four secular canons had been stationed in Daventry, and with the erection of the new building, two retained their secular role while the others became monks. Over the years the number of monks attached to the Daventry site increased, and by the 14th century there were eighteen. Not only did they have use of the original buildings, but they also acquired a good deal of land, together with other buildings, and so became quite wealthy.

When the Bishop paid a visit to the town in 1442, it is recorded that the Prior, by the name of Robert, was not quite what he should have been, and he was accused of a variety of crimes, including simony (buying and selling ecclesiastical promotion/privileges), incompetence in temporal administration and adultery with Agnes Mason of Daventry. In spite of the charges, we do not know what punishment, if any, was meted out because there is no record. If he was punished, he certainly was not drummed out of his position, because four years later he was still the Prior.

Various developments took place over succeeding centuries, and at one time it appears that there were apparently two churches, an assumption made from references to the 'parochial nave' and the 'parochial chancel'. At this time Daventry was in the Diocese of Lincoln, and the Bishop was concerned about this situation, so he informed the parishioners and monks that there should only be one church. To bring about this unity he instructed them to build a new church that would be big enough to take in the parochial high altar that at the time stood in the middle of the church. For several centuries, and particularly from references in documents covering the period 1300–1600, the church became known as 'The Church of St Augustine'. However, there is also mention of the term 'Holy Cross' way back in 1240, and other documentary evidence suggests that this refers to the parochial part of the church, further strengthening the two-church situation.

> *Some historians have pointed out that the reason for having two churches may have been due to the fact that when the monks separated, each group had their own dedication for the building. Anther suggestion as to the inclusion of the name 'Holy Cross' is that during Saxon times, church dedications in general include 'Holy Cross' and 'Holy Rood', so the dedication may even have been there when the monks first arrived – though it is impossible to prove this.*

In the 18th century it is known there was a Gothic tower at the west end of the north aisle, and the rest of the building consisted of a nave with north and south aisles. The tower also used to be adorned with pinnacles. In his 18th century historical survey, Bridges was less than complementary about the interior of the Daventry church, saying that it consisted of "a clutter of pews and galleries". His other notes also give a clue to the earlier building, because he refers to an arcade of square pillars which were on the north side, suggesting this part of the building originated prior to the Norman Conquest. He contrasts this with the south side where there were round pillars, suggesting links to the 13th century.

With the increasing number of coaches passing through Daventry in the early part of the 18th century there was an expansion in the population, necessitating extensions to the church. The five bells were expanded to a peal of eight in 1738, and other work included the erection of a number of galleries. However, it was not long before the authorities realised that these additions only added to the unsatisfactory nature of the church, which by this time was showing its age, due in no small measure to poor maintenance in the past. Not only were many parts of the building literally falling down, but other areas were also dangerous to would-be worshippers. To add to this general deterioration, a fire late in the 17th century apparently also caused much damage to various parts of the building, including the windows, tower and roof.

Early in 1752, the combined might of the clergy, the town's aldermen, worshippers and inhabitants voiced their concerns about the state of the building to the Bishop of Peterborough, and went as far as to suggest that the church should be demolished, and that a new building be erected where the previous church had stood. It was obvious that people were aware of the problems, and at the time of the petition their support was evident because £2000 had already been raised. The Bishop arranged for a commission to visit Daventry so that the concerns of both parishioners and other residents could be aired. The meeting was held in the Swan Inn, opposite the church, rather than in the church building – in view of its dangerous nature. During its visit, the Commission took statements from a number of people, one of whom was a carpenter brought in to carry out repairs to the church which he did, to quote from the report, "to the hazard of his life". During the submissions, the commissioners collected enough evidence from the local inhabitants to convince the Bishop of their concerns, because the Ipiscopal Seal – dated 9 February 1752 – was affixed to the faculty for rebuilding the church.

David Hiorne from Warwick, whose style was influenced by a number of notable architects, including James Gibbs, the architect responsible for St Martins-in-the Fields in London, designed the existing church. His father, a builder also from Warwick, had given evidence to the church commission about the state of the present building. On 8 April 1752, two months after the faculty had been signed, the foundation stone was laid. The new church was erected on the site of the former building, the architect using a similar ground plan. Within two years, all the pew rentals had been agreed. Perhaps not surprisingly, the best pews were allocated to those who had provided the most cash when it came to the rebuilding fund. It took six years before the building was completed, although the first Sunday Service took place on 13 October 1754. Northamptonshire brown ironstone was used for the construction, and the total cost was £3486. 2. 5 1/2, which included the bells and chimes.

The porch leads into the entrance lobby. Although many might dismiss this in their haste to get into the main part of the church building, it is worth taking a look at the large oak 'Dole Cupboard' on the south side, which bears the names of the churchwardens at the time of the building's erection.

The term 'dole' refers to the bread and other food that was kept there for distribution to the poor.

Once inside the church there is an air of space, and the lofty exterior is carried into the building. The Doric pillars in the nave and aisles are not solid stone, but are constructed from wood coated with plaster. There are two fonts, the earlier dating from 1840, the portable one from 1990 (the latter was made and given by a student from Danetre – then Southbrook – School). The Lady Chapel is a new addition, having been formed when three pews were taken out.

There are galleries on the north and south side of the church, and these have had few alterations made to them since they were installed. However, the west gallery was made level and screening added in 1974, and at the same time the north staircase was blocked. This gallery is used for coffee after some services, and also for breakfast after Sunday Eucharist. On the south side, behind the gallery, there is a kitchen, and on the north side an office. Two features hidden from most visitors are the windows, one in the kitchen and the other in the office. Although small, they have some very fine decorative glass. The Arms of the Earl of Winchelsea, the Lord of the Manor, are shown on one. The other bears the arms of Christ Church, Oxford that are ensigned with a cardinal's hat (the cardinal's hat sits above the arms). This window has links with the 1526 dissolution of the Priory. The glass itself is much later, and was probably fashioned just before the new church was started. Hidden, as these windows are, the information depicted on the glass is important because it is a timely reminder of the history of both the present church and earlier Priory.

In the chancel the pulpit, together with the two clergy stalls, are believed to be original, although it is possible they may once have formed a three-decker pulpit. The reredos behind the altar dates from 1920, and is worth closer scrutiny. It shows the Resurrection, with archangels Gabriel and Raphael. These two figures are relatively new, and replaced the Lord's Prayer, the Ten Commandments and the Creed. Apart from the windows off the west gallery, those in the aisles add to the attractiveness of the building. With the exception of The Good Shepherd in the south aisle, they are painted, rather than being fashioned from stained glass. The south aisle window was erected in memory of Blanche Isobel Campbell, who was burnt to death in 1928. In the chancel there is a Venetian window above this altar, produced by Wailes in 1860. The Ascension is shown in the centre, with the Baptism of Christ in the Jordan and the Magi on either side. The original roof was altered in 1986, when the wood was replaced with stainless steel.

The church has a peal of ten bells, and seven of these are the work of Thomas Earye of Kettering. Dated 1738, they were transferred from the old church. There is a further bell, dated 1764, produced by Joseph Earye, a brother of Thomas, whose bellfoundry was in St. Neots. As with most other churches, work has been carried out on the bells since the new church was built. During the 20th century, work has been undertaken at the modern bellfoundry of James Taylor & Co, Loughborough, including recasting, with major activity having taken place in 1965. The present peal of ten bells was hung in a new frame in 1965, when three of the bells were recast and two new trebles added to those already there. Earyes of Kettering were also responsible for the original clock that was produced in 1757. With modernisation a new electric clock was installed in 1965, to replace the earlier mechanical model. The Kettering firm also produced a chiming machine, and this continued to be used until the middle of this century. The chiming machine had a different tune for each weekday and two for Sundays, each being played at three hourly intervals.

The parish registers, now at the County Record Office for safe keeping, go back to 1560. A collection of books – many in Latin, and of 16th century origin – are still part of the church's collection, and are kept in the building.

> Although the Local Ecumenical Project covenant was not signed until the 1980s, one bell includes the line Do nothing separately that may be done together; this is incorporated into the Covenant.

daventry
methodist church

No one is quite certain when Methodism came to Daventry, but research carried out by John Follett seems to suggest that 1797 was the likely date when groups of non-conformists, following Wesley's tradition, met in the town. Reports from the time suggest that fourteen people met, most of whom were men. At this stage there would have been no building for this worship, even though a congregational church (now the URC) had already been built.

The first Methodist – a Wesleyan – society met in a house that was licensed in 1797. According to some sources, the group came into being partly as a result of Unitarianism among some of the students at the Doddridge Academy which met at Sheaf Street in the town.

It is not known for certain when the first Methodist Church was built, though there were at least two other churches prior to the present 1974 building. Sources suggest that the first church was in what was known, appropriately, as Chapel Lane, which later became St John's Square. A report in the Methodist Recorder of 24 March 1930 indicates that a Wesleyan Chapel preceded the then new one in New Street, and the writer of the article states "...I made careful enquiries in Chapel Lane, but could not discover any remains of the old building which was used for many years as a mineral water factory". However, the town had Methodist Ministers before the second chapel was constructed, and it was a Circuit in its own right with the first Minister, the Rev. Thomas Stanton, serving from 1806.

The second chapel was built in what is now New Street, which at the time was called Cow Lane. Erected in 1824, its broad three-bay front had a pedimental gable, together with arched upper windows. That building was compulsorily purchased in 1966 as a result of overspill arrangements with Birmingham City Council in the 1970s, but it has not been demolished and is still is use today. At present, the building is used for a variety of purposes: one section is used a nightclub, and other parts of the buildings are occupied by the Day Centre, with the VIP Club using an upstairs room for their recording studios, where they produce the monthly *VIP Sound*, a tape for Visually Impaired People.

The present church, built on land in Golding Close, was opened in September 1974, some 150 years after the New Street Church. The building soon became too small for an expanding congregation, and since its inauguration two extensions have been added. The first came in 1978 in the form of a multi-purpose stage room, and was added to the hall; the second was a two-storey extension with a new entrance porch, additional foyer area, lounge and upstairs meeting room, which came into use in 1992. The foundation stone bears the following wording: *This building erected in 1974 continues the work of the church in New Street which for 150 years witnessed to the Glory of God.*

It is worth visiting this modern building for the display of banners, produced by an active Banner Group. The number of highly attractive designs continues to increase, and hanging in the main worship building they enhance the bare brick walls, and bring an added dimension to worship. Texts and themes include 'Love one another as I have loved you', 'He leads me be side still waters', and 'The leaves of the tree are for the healing of the nations'. There are also two modern stones with Biblical inscriptions carved by Harold Crossley at the age of 87.

> *Apart from Sunday worship, the church is used for numerous activities, including classes and groups from both the church and surrounding town. The church is open during the morning from Monday to Thursday for refreshments.*

daventry
roman catholic church

Following the 16th century Reformation, life became extremely different for Roman Catholics, and most lived in fear of persecution. Services, including mass, became secret meetings. Priests were lodged in what became known as 'safe houses'. Parliamentary legislation reaching the statue books in 1791 made things easier, and this was reinforced by the Catholic Emancipation Act in 1829. From then on, Catholics were no longer victimised and were once more allowed to take public office. Because of the influx of Irish regiments to the army barracks at Weedon, a Roman Catholic Priest used a room in the building so that individuals serving with the army could take mass.

In 1880, the Roman Catholic Church came to Daventry when a house and land was purchased in London Road. A Roman Catholic Priest used the building as a Presbytery, and one room became a chapel. Buildings at the rear were eventually enlarged, and a chapel dedicated to St Mark opened. This marked a turning point for Roman Catholicism in Daventry.

The number of Roman Catholics continued to grow, and the sixty-seater chapel became inadequate, so the group moved to the old 17th century grammar school in New Street. The building was dedicated to 'Our Lady of Charity and St. Augustine', the same title as the earlier dedication of the Priory. Although originally leased, the Church eventually bought the building in 1924.

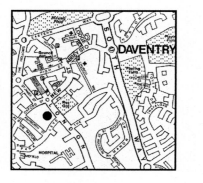

With the continuing growth in Daventry's population the New Street Church became too small, and negotiations were begin into 1962 to find new premises. The current church in London Road is on the site of the former Fox and Hounds inn, and building work began in 1971. Eventually a dual-purpose church was dedicated in 1972. Further work was started on the site in 1989 to provide a large hall, and at the same time alterations were made to the existing building. The present building, with its open layout, is not a modern design, but based on the early Greek meeting halls, where the first Christians met.

daventry
united reformed church

The current United Reformed Church is the oldest non-conformist church in Daventry. Situated in Sheaf Street, the present meeting house was acquired in 1723, and this was placed in trust. The building that faces Sheaf Street is situated just off it, and is entered through an arch, along a passageway formed from the buildings on either side. Above the building there is a tablet, which was erected in 1864, and which bears the words "Independent Chapel Erected AD 1722".

The chapel, built of rubble walls and with a hipped tiled roof, was altered in 1959. The south-west front, with its six bays and two tiers of windows, was covered with rendering towards the end of the last century. During these alterations, the doorways – which were to both the left and right of the building – were re-positioned, and now form a central entrance.

The rear wall of the original chapel is now lost, as it was covered with other buildings, forming the Foundry Place Rooms – which also belong to the church. There were two windows on either side of the pulpit, but these were blocked in when development took place behind the building. The upper windows still remain in the gallery. The side walls have three bays, each of which has two tiers of windows.

There are two central timber posts in the interior, supporting a valley-beam which runs parallel to the front. These posts are circular with octagonal bases, and feature small moulded capitals. The gallery, which was almost completely rebuilt in the 19th century, stretches around three sides of the building. At the same time a great deal of other building work was carried out.

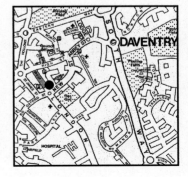

The seating plan of 1775 is interesting because it shows that there was only one gallery at the south-west end, the side galleries being added in about 1820. The pulpit, of hexagonal design, is fitted with panelled sides and a staircase that has twisted balusters, and is from the 18th century.

dodford
church of st mary

Travelling along the busy A45, whether from Weedon or from the Daventry direction, the tower of the Church of St. Mary in Dodford is conspicuous, and from the road at least is a particularly distinctive feature of this small village. Tucked away in the folds of the Northamptonshire countryside amidst narrow lanes – and with both old and new developments sitting comfortably side by side – somehow it has survived the ravages of past centuries intact.

Strolling down a narrow road, flanked on either side by steep grassy banks, the church comes into view on the edge of the village, still surrounded by rolling open countryside as it has been since it was first built – although it is only in relatively recent times that its tranquillity has been disturbed by the roar of traffic along the busy A45. Cattle graze lazily in some of the surrounding fields, adding to the tranquillity.

There was almost certainly some kind of building in the area prior to the 13th century, because some fragments have survived from an earlier period. These can be found on the exterior south wall close to the most easterly window. Here two distinct areas of herringbone masonry are evident which, according to historians, are probably remnants from Saxon times. Whether the bricks came from an earlier church or other building, no one is certain. The tower at the west end of the building carries the imprints of 13th century craftsmen. Lacking battlements, the structure is nevertheless enhanced by attractive pinnacles emerging from each corner. A peal of six bells hang within the tower, five of which bear a variety of 17th century dates, the exception being the treble.

The two-storey south porch, from the Perpendicular period, has heavy rib vaulting. Above this there was an upper room which has been completely blocked off, making it inaccessible. Step inside the building through the south door, with its single lancet window, and a substantial 13th century arch confronts the visitor. Despite the fact that there is only one aisle, on the north, the nave is wide, giving the church a feeling of spaciousness.

42

Like the tower, the nave was also built in the 13th century. The two Norman windows have ornamental zigzag plaster work on the inside, and the high nave clerestory is enhanced with an array of plain coloured glass.

Philip Hardwick was responsible for re-building the chancel in 1850, and William Butterfield then restored it, together with the nave, between 1878 and 1880.

Within the small, Victorian vestry, some fine Jacobean panels have been incorporated into panelling carried out in more recent times. Like so many buildings, it is the radiant stained glass in the east window of the chancel and the small lancet-shaped west window of the tower that attracts the eye. The latter shows Mary holding the infant Jesus, and was given to the Church by Mary and William Thompson in memory of their daughter, Mavis Lilian Thompson, a baby born in 1686 and who died in the same year.

The glass is the east window of the north aisle shows nativity scenes, and was put in place in 1876 in memory of the Hewitt family. Anne is in the centre, Richard (their son) to her left, and her husband Robert to the right. The central light features a stable scene with Mary watching over the infant Jesus in his stall. The left light shows the angel visiting the shepherds, contrasting with that on the right side where the Epiphany scene depicts the three wise men bearing gifts for the young baby. The work of Clutterbuck can be seen in the glass in the east window, reflecting the style of both German and Dutch 16th century stained glass.

Although most of the north aisle was built in the 13th century, William de Keynes added to this as part of the extensive restoration work he undertook. It is in this part of the church that many fine earlier monuments have been placed in memory of a number of the past Lords of the Manor. The oldest of these has been fashioned from Purbeck stone, and features a superb carving of a cross-legged knight, and is to the memory of Robert de Keynes, who died in 1305.

The church also contains other interesting monuments. There is a fascinating oak effigy, partially hidden behind a tomb chest, and dedicated to the memory of Hawise de Keynes. Carved around 1280 from one piece of oak, it

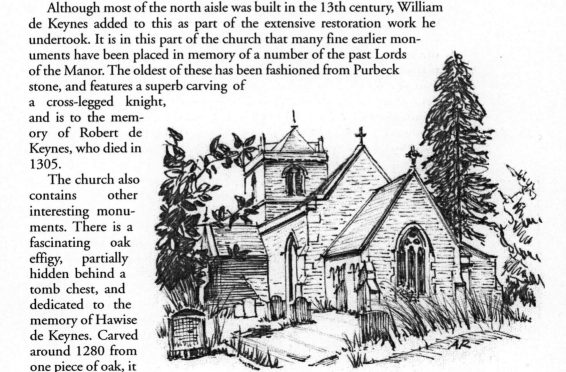

is not surprising that it has been ravaged by dry rot, fungus and death watch beetle. Restoration work has been assisted by grants from the Council for Places of Worship and by other organisations and individuals outside the parish. In addition to the main carving, it also features five small mourners. A later relative, Sir Robert de Keynes, who died in about 1305, is resplendent in his Purbeck marble effigy in the form of a cross-legged knight. Here he rests on a slab that closely resembles a tapering coffin lid.

> *Perhaps for many visitors the most intriguing effigy can be seen on the tomb chest of what is said to be Wentiliana de Keynes, who died in 1376. She lies in a rebuilt and restored coffer tomb. She is wearing a flowing dress, her head rests on a pillow, and her hands are clasped in prayer. The carving also shows that angels guard her. Around the sides of her coffin are five weepers. Historians believe she is probably the great, great granddaughter of Hawise.*

As with many earlier churches, Dodford also has brass memorials, two of which date from the 15th century, and which can be seen in the chancel. The oldest of these commemorates the life of Sir John Cressy, who died in 1414; it also shows his wife. The second brass is to William Wylde and his wife, and dates from 1422.

A later Sir John Cressy, who died in 1444, has a free-standing alabaster monument in which he is shown as a recumbent figure. He wears a hauberk (coat) of ringed mail, and has one of his hands resting on his scabbard, with the other, by its position, appearing to have just reached back to the sword. Two kneeling angels support his head, and there are more angels, also holding shields. In the arched panels between them are figures of small mourners.

The circular Norman font is also a distinctive feature of St Mary's Church, and has richly decorated Norman lunettes, semi-circular decorations. Cressy donated the rood screen, which features one-light divisions. Just to the south of the rood screen and above the lady altar is a painted statue of the Blessed Lady dating from the 15th century.

A board on the north wall of the tower gives details about the Dodford Charitable Endowments of Cook and Thornton and Freeman and King. The piscina in the east wall of the north aisle is close to where an earlier altar once stood. The pews in the sanctuary have some good example of poppy head carvings.

everdon
church of st mary

There are delightful – even tantalising – views of this large parish church from almost every direction as you enter the village – whether it is when it comes into view from the Farthingstone and Weedon directions – or where it stands secluded on a rise in the hollow seen over the narrow road from Fawsley. Like the church, the village also nestles in a hollow, but as with so many churches, St. Mary's stands sentinel on a higher point.

The earliest parts of the present church date from the 14th century, but it is possible that there was a church on the site prior to this. Built during the reign of Edward III (1327–1377) in Decorated style, the list of incumbents reveals that Elias Capellinus de Everdone was appointed in 1218, which may suggest that some sort of structure was in place at this time, and possibly earlier. The only remaining relic of an earlier church may be the font, though as with many other religious houses, this could have been brought to the village at a later date. If an earlier building existed, its position and date of demolition remain a mystery.

In this pleasant village, whose name means 'boar's hill' (eofor = boar, dun = hill), such a large church in so small community generally causes some amazement. But as the story unfolds, the reason for such a big building becomes clear. Inside, visitors can only marvel at the space – it is undoubtedly to earlier wealthy benefactors that the present building owes its existence. It is certain that at least some of the earlier inhabitants, like those in surrounding settlements, were involved in the then lucrative wool trade, and the money for building came from this. For such a small village, with a population of around 350, the upkeep of the church is a major headache. Thousands of pounds have already been raised during the last twenty or so years, and plans are in hand to raise a further £250,000.

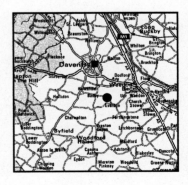

The building was founded by monks who came over from Bernay in France. Since Everdon had connections with the Abbey at Bernay, this link is not unreasonable. In turn, the French brought their own stonemasons by the name of de Corville to carry out the master plan. Although the name de Corville has long vanished from the electoral registers, it is thought to remain in what has been corrupted to Carvell, and many members of the family with that name inhabited the village during the earlier part of the 20th century.

The west tower has four 'Y' shaped bell openings and a pinnacled parapet, with distinctive RY weather vanes on each corner. The five bells, now more than 500 years old, still hang in the ancient oak frame. Three of the bells bear the date 1625, the fourth 1626, and the fifth 1635. Restoration took place in 1889, and again in 1976, but the weight of the bells is such that ringing is no longer possible. Funds are being raised to ensure that the bells can once again be rung over this part of the county.

> *The letters RY always cause debate. Could they stand for the first letters of Richard Knightley? Did the person who made them get it wrong and the Y should have been a K for Knightley?*

Additions have been made over the years which have enlarged the original church, but it still retains a great deal of its early 14th century architecture, including both north and south doorways, the north aisle, east window, west tower and south aisle windows. The window at the east end of the south aisle is particularly interesting, and features some unusual tracery. The church's north porch is reached along a short path, through a churchyard with ancient yews and lime trees. Entrance is through the north doorway, opposite which is the 14th century south doorway – described by Pevsner as "sumptuous" – which has intricate carving worth a look. Arched, with rows of flowery carvings, including foliage and ballflowers, there are also three concentric steps (orders) of wedge-shaped stones (*voussoirs*) which get smaller towards the opening. Above there is a leafy crested arch, ending in two heads, one representing a bishop.

From the exterior, the size of the building suggests one of internal space, which is confirmed once inside. The nave, lofty and massive, adds to this feeling of spaciousness. The four arches on each side of the nave rise until they meet the clerestory windows. Stretch the neck and it's possible to make out one or two wooden corbels which formed part of the original roof; these have been carved with comic head features. Enjoy the beautiful 14th tracery in the lofty aisle windows. The original glass in the east window of the south aisle has been replaced with modern material, and several angels are represented, including the Archangel Gabriel wearing a folded robe, the Archangel Michael resplendent in shining armour, St. Stephen clothed in green, and St. Alban wearing a blue outfit.

> *Although Northamptonshire stone gives the building a delightfully warm glow, which in turn adds to the charm of the church, it erodes very easily, which has caused, and still causes, many problems to those responsible for the building's upkeep. Where harder oolite limestone has been used, for example in the windows, this is much more durable, and shows only slight signs of weathering.*

The central arch and six bays of the 14th century chancel screen are magnificently carved with fine tracery. The comic heads on the cusps almost touch each other, and a variety of other carvings, including dragons and winged lions, are worth looking for in the lower panels.

The rood screen separates the nave from the chancel and is of medieval origin. With its ogee arches, above which is intricate tracery, it is a good example – at least when compared to other pieces in Northamptonshire. The octagonal font, which stands at the western end of the nave, is carved from Purbeck marble, and is 13th century in origin. It is possible that it might be the only remaining item from an earlier church, but this is pure speculation as it could have been brought from elsewhere.

In the sanctuary on the south side altar there is a 15th century tomb recess which has an ogee head. It has been suggested that this was intended for the tomb of the founder. On the north wall there is a simply fashioned sedilia which has ogee arches, above which are crocketted gables. An interesting small brass in the sanctuary bears the date 1655, and provides details about Rev. Timothy Dod, one of Everdon's former rectors, who was buried there. Timothy's claim to fame included the size of his frame, which made it impossible for him to preach from St Mary's pulpit. He was a popular figure, and was so respected that the local people increased his stipend to £50 a year, When offered this increase in his income Dod, conscious of poverty in the area, told those involved that he would only accept it if it wasn't collected from the poor of the parish.

Lacking in fine monuments, the church has a number of wall tablets. One on the south side of the chancel arch is to the memory of Thomas Spencer, who died in 1606, and the tablet has heraldic emblems. Both the Spencer, of Althorp and the Knightleys of Fawsley have associations with the church.

As in many churches, there is often an air of mystery, and this is true for St. Mary's. The balcony that crosses the nave at the west end of the church has given rise to much speculation, and a several theories have been proposed to explain its existence. One idea was that the monks used it to gain access to the roof, keeping the inhabitants informed of would-be enemies. But although fascinating, this has generally

been dismissed – it was probably built to give access to the church roofs; not for the monks, but for those who maintained the building. The present balcony is of relatively recent origin, having been built in 1892. Close scrutiny of the balustrade also suggests that it is 19th century, which means that it also dates from the same period.

It is known that as a child the poet Thomas Gray came to stay with his uncle William Antrobus, who was Rector of Everdon. Some people like to let their imagination run wild, and suggest that it was Everdon – rather than Stokes Poges – which inspired Gray's *Elegy in an English Churchyard.* Leave the church and wander round to the north side and stand in the graveyard, and here in the relative peace of this quiet Northamptonshire village read the first verse of the poem.

> *The curfew tolls the knell of parting day*
> *The lowing herd winds slowly o'er the lea*
> *The ploughman homeward plods his weary way*
> *And leaves the world to darkness and to me.*

Now allow your eyes to wander over the fields into the distance, and somehow it almost seems to ring true. Look at other verses to see what you think. And while in the churchyard, you might also be interested in an earlier event. In the 13th century, when Oliver Sutton was Bishop of Ely, someone was murdered in this sacred ground – but no one is quite certain as to what actually happened, although it is known that in 1293 Sutton granted a commission to the priory of Daventry to reconcile it.

farthingstone
church of st mary the virgin

Farthingstone, or Faxastun to the locals, is a small, charming, picturesque and unspoilt Northamptonshire village, with a collection of mainly ironstone buildings. With its main street, little development has taken place in recent years, though some infilling has featured and some older buildings have been converted. The small Norman church, reached through a lych gate, dates from about 1200. The west tower, relatively squat and without buttresses, is embellished with four substantial pinnacles, one on each corner. The door in the south wall of the tower obviously gave access in the past, though is probably only now used in emergencies. The ring of five bells in the tower includes three dated 1633 and two from 1822.

Access is through the south porch, with its customary footscraper close by, an obligatory piece of equipment in days past! The oak porch gates were given in memory of Miss Barbara Adams – entrance into the church is through the studded south door.

Even though Farthingstone is a quiet village, off the beaten track, there is an even greater air of calm and peace inside the compact building. The only noise is the consistent thud of the clock in the bell tower. The time-piece was produced by J. Smith of Derby in 1873, and is a 'weekly winder'. The interior tower arch is of simple design, and dates from the same period as the tower.

The original chancel owes its existence to late 13th craftsmen, and features interesting sedilia, together with a tomb recess that exhibits an ogee arch to the west – an unusual position for this particular feature, as it is often found on the south wall of the chancel.

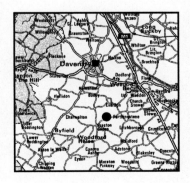

The nave has a small aisle, which might be considered a chapel, complete with a 13th century arch featuring a respond and a stiff leaf capital. The pews are interesting with their carvings of oak leaves and acorns. For the size of the church, the tub font, to the west of the nave, is quite large, and is early 13th century in origin. The plain door in the outer north wall also dates from the earliest part of the church, above which is a memorial to members of the Shepherd family.

The benches, with their ornate poppy heads, stand in the nave, and are of great age. These are worth closer investigation, and feature a variety of designs, including a winged demon playing a drum, peeping over his shoulder a playful kitten. At the same time, a monkey happily bashes together some cymbals, whilst an owl mournfully plays a pipe. To complete the musical ensemble, a donkey rattles a tambourine! In addition, one pew is carved with a beautiful floral design. It seems that the carver had a sense of humour, as he placed a serpent near the Rector's pew! The stone reredos dates from the Victorian era, and is almost certainly a result of the restorative work that took place at that time.

The stained glass windows, some of which were produced in the 13th century, add to the overall attraction of the building. However, there is also much later, equally attractive, glass. At the west end of the nave the windows show four knights from Arthur's Round Table, erected in memory of members of the Agnew family who died in the 1914–1918 war. To the east of the south door there is a window commemorating the life of Enid Jocelyn (Joy) Agnew, who died in 1911. The delightfully executed scene shows her surrounded by small pink roses, with colourful birds above her head. The Joymead Garden sited in the village also commemorates Joy Agnew.

The Agnew family moved into the village in the 1920s, and Philip Agnew, JP – although he held no official title – was looked upon as the squire. At one time he held the office of High Sheriff of Northamptonshire. He was also the proprietor of the satirical magazine Punch. *His family suffered many tragedies, and his daughter, Enid Jocelyn – known affectionately as Joy – died at the age of 22. His son, Lieutenant Ewan Siegfried, a member of the 5th Royal Irish Lancers, was killed during World War I.*

Miss Grant of Litchborough gave the east window in memory of her father and brother. The organ sits in the Chapel of St Anne, dedicated to the mother of the Virgin Mary.

During the 19th century some restoration and rebuilding work took place. This activity in 1852 was followed in 1874, some 20 years later, with further work on the chancel, and it was at this time that the vestry was also built.

fawsley
church of st mary

Innumerable adjectives – lonely, isolated, deserted, remote, solitary – spring to mind when Fawsley Church first appears in view. The church, situated on a slight rise in the middle of a meadow, begs the question "Why here?" It takes a search into the history books and an understanding of the Knightleys of Fawsley to realise that here, within sight of this 13th century church, was not one, but possibly two, thriving communities. Such was the importance of Fawsley in the past that the whole area was known as Fawsley Hundred, just as the area around Daventry is now known as Daventry District.

The history of the area is fascinating in itself, but at this stage, all that needs to be said is that, due to pressures from the Knightley family in the 16th and 17th centuries, the people left Fawsley, and the Knightleys were able to fence the land for the productive activity of sheep-farming. Today the church still survives in splendid isolation amidst the lakes and parkland so lovingly created by Capability Brown, one of Britain's greatest landscape gardeners. But for some 400 years its history has been inextricably linked with the family that once occupied the building that is but a (long) stone's throw from the religious house. Here the church shares remnants of the past with Fawsley Hall, now a hotel, bearing testimony to the residency of one of Northamptonshire's great families. Here too, according to the history books, Queen Elizabeth I stayed on her journey to Kenilworth Castle, and here too – in more tragic circumstances – John Merrick (the Elephant Man) found respite on the estate. Charles I also enjoyed hunting deer – so we are told – in Badby Wood before the fateful Battle of Naseby, and within walking distance of St. Mary's Church.

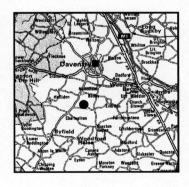

Having walked across the field, the lichen encrusted church is surrounded by a feature called a ha-ha. This sunken ditch was dug out as a deterrent for keeping sheep out of the churchyard, which is still used for burials. There are one or two memorials to the Knightleys and their workers, including one to a waggoner, but most to the illustrious family are inside the building.

No one is certain whether there was a church on the site prior to the 13th century building, but it has been suggested that there may have been a wooden Saxon structure. Founded in the 13th century, Fawsley is probably one of the most visited of Northamptonshire's small village churches, with its links not only with the Knightleys, but also with the Washingtons.

In Decorated style, several corbels arranged around the parapet enhance the squat west steepleless tower, also dating from the 13th century. Stare at them for a while and it becomes obvious that some have strange, animal-like shapes. Stand facing the tower, and above the west window there is an ogee niche which – as far as is known – once housed a statue of Our Blessed Lady.

Cross the bridge over the ha-ha and step through the low north doorway into the church, perhaps suggesting that people then were smaller than today. Once inside, the light which floods in through the plain glass high in the clerestory windows immediately strikes you. But even this flood of light is not enough in the winter for services, and both lighting and heating were added in the spring of 1999. A cursory glance not only reveals a fine south door, with its external porch, a nave, two aisles and a chancel, but also the innumerable monuments.

As with many churches, changes have taken place over the years. A superb 15th century roof protects the original 13th century nave. Having survived for more than four centuries, including the inevitable attention of innumerable timber-boring beetles in that time, it is now in fine shape, having been treated for death watch beetle during the 1960s. Sadly, the roof seldom attracts much attention, but it is worth spending a few minutes gazing upwards to appreciate the original and richly decorated hammer beams.

The nave, of 13th century origin, possesses two three-bay arcades, each with octagonal arches. One of the greatest problems with churches was the entry of enough natural light. This must have been the case with Fawsley, and during either the 16th or 17th century – four or five centuries after the earliest part of the first building – large clear-glass clerestory windows were fitted. Today they are still important for lighting the church for visitors, but their use for services has been superseded by man-made lighting.

The low box pews, for the common parishioners, are located in the nave and two aisles at the west end of the church, with higher ones used by the upper class in the south aisle and nearer to the altar. Although the taller squire's pew dates from the 17th century, it is of relatively little interest because of its plain woodwork. Nevertheless, there is an interesting squint through the wall on the eastern side of the chancel arch. With these tall pews, the Knightley family could not be seen by the rest of the congregation, but they were able to see when communion was taking place, and so be able to participate in the activities at the altar rail.

If these Knightley pews are of relatively little interest, attention soon focuses on the other finely carved and superbly restored 16th century furniture. There have been many suggestions as to the interpretation of the various carvings, but it is generally agreed that it was the woodcarver's subtle way of reflecting on the social activities of the time. It has also been suggested that nursery rhymes are to be seen, and if this is so, then they too are a reflection of the social nature of that period.

Music in the church has long been provided by an original 1822 barrel organ, which was later modified and fitted with a keyboard and pedals. Three hatchments hanging on the nave walls, have recently been returned to the church after restoration.

Standing in the north aisle, the font has seen better days, although it is of ancient lineage. Dating from the 13th century, the original carving has clearly deteriorated considerably, and it has since been re-worked.

Stained glass windows in many parts of the building reflect the dedication and skill of earlier craftsmen. The oldest of these is the tiny west window behind the vestry, a curtained area near the bell tower. According to historians, the

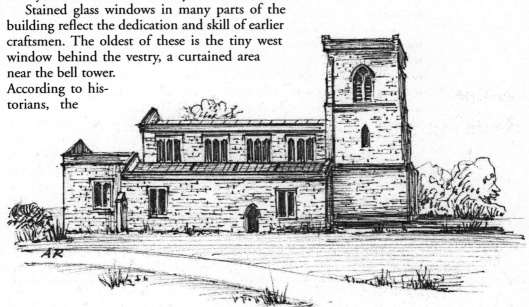

HATCHMENTS

Diamond-shaped hatchments originated in the low countries, but their use was changed once they crossed the channel. In British traditions a hatchment was carried in front of the funeral procession. After burial, it was taken back to the house where it was hung, often outside, during the period of mourning. This over, it was taken back to the church as a permanent reminder of the deceased.

glass in this window is 13th century in origin, and a close examination shows two characters, purported to be Adam and Eve in the Garden of Eden. At first sight, the most striking window is that in the east wall, above the altar, and the new glass replaces an older window shown on a painting hanging on the west wall of the tower. This east window dates from 1866, and is in memory of Sir Charles and Lady Knightley. He is adorned in a blue mantle, scarlet hunting suit and white breeches; his wife is wearing a blue hooded cloak. The window is worth closer investigation, portraying as it does a Biblical scene from the Book of Ruth.

Other windows are also of interest, and some Washington heraldic devices in the east windows of both the north and south aisles were brought from Sulgrave Manor, to the south of Fawsley, in 1830. It is possible to see the stars and stripes, a feature in the Washington coat of arms, and which were used when the American flag was designed.

It is worth spending some time looking at the nave windows. They consist of 15th century Flemish glass, and depict a number of scenes including Christ on his Way to Jerusalem, the Good Samaritan, the Last Supper and the Crucifixion.

Fawsley Church is full of treasures, and the stone Bible on the window ledge in the east window of the north aisle is no exception. But in spite of all this, it is the Knightley memorials that are undoubtedly the most striking feature of this small, isolated church. There are no fewer than fifteen, spanning a period from 1516 to 1856. The oldest is the 18 in (45cm) high brass of a knight, situated on the floor of the nave, just in front of the tower arch. A fascinating memorial, it shows Thomas Knightley, and not only his heraldry, but also his heart, engraved above his portrait. Other memorials feature various members of the Knightley family through succeeding generations. The most distinctive is the free-standing alabaster tomb commemorating Sir Richard Knightley and his wife, Jane Skennard. Both are shown in prayer, and the tomb also features their children on either side. Dating from 1534, the tomb also has weepers – eight sons on one side and four daughters on the other.

A book is available at the church which gives more information about various aspects of the church and park.

flecknoe
church of st mark

This small Warwickshire hilltop village has a history that was first recorded in the Domesday Survey, at which time it was part of the Turchill of Arden estate, within the parish of Wolfhampscote. Although the estate of Turchill disappeared long ago, its position within the same parish remains. In size it would have been considered quite a substantial settlement, with a population of around 110. Over the centuries there have been many ups and down in the fortunes of Flecknoe, and today's population is not that much different from the one recorded during the 1086 Domesday Survey. A recent move has suggested that what remains from an earlier age should be preserved, and a monument, 'Medieval settlement remains in Flecknoe', is to be instigated by English Heritage. English Heritage indicate that there was a chapel in the village by 1360, but whether this was the same building which Dugdale recorded as a "decayed chapel" in the 17th century is not known

How long the chapel was in use also remains a mystery, but for some time villagers from Flecknoe made the relatively short journey of a couple of miles to the nearby parish church of Wolfhamcote. There is a little confusion here, because the village is called Wolfhamcote; the parish Wolfhampcote! But the tide changed, and the church that came into being in Flecknoe appeared almost by accident. When the railway came to the area, the company offered compensation because the vicarage was to be disturbed. The new vicarage was erected in Flecknoe, as there was no longer a settlement at Wolfhamcote.

When the vicarage was completed it was found there was £1000 left, enough to build a simple red brick building, and in 1891 the Church of St Mark was erected. The building was used for worship from time to time, but main worship continued at Wolfhamcote.

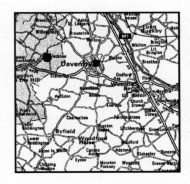

The path leads past a small part of the churchyard, which has an interesting gravestone with a sheep on the top. Entrance is through the west porch, built in 1989 to replace an earlier one. The purpose of the new brick structure was to help support the walls of the church

building, but this has only been partially successfully, as it has put a strain on the corner of the main building. Having entered the building through the west door, and in spite of its relatively simple nature, the church is attractive, with the east window and south wall flooded with stained glass. The plain brick walls have been left because of problems with cracking, and plastering would not be satisfactory. Due to the problems of shrinkage, some windows have been reset. The building consists of a nave and a chancel, with a vestry on the south side and an organ chamber on the north. The stand-alone organ came from Priors Marston, and it was unveiled at the Feast of St Lawrence in 1910.

> *The church of St. Mark in Flecknoe has the distinction of being the smallest church in the Diocese of Warwick. With relatively little money, not only was the new building a simple structure, but it was built on clay and on shallow foundations – not a good combination! The clay causes many problems. During the summer, when the clay dries out, large cracks appear in certain parts of the building. These lessen again in winter.*

Apart from its simple construction, the joy of the church is undoubtedly its stained glass windows, which are arranged in pairs and have various quotations from the bible: "As ye have done it unto one of these least of these my brethren ye have done it unto me", in the east end of the south wall, to illustrations of St. Matthew and St. Mark. The westerly window on the same wall bears the text "To be a light to lighten the Gentiles and to be the glory of thy people Israel". Two in the chancel show Faith and Hope, with Charity being positioned above the west door. The stained glass windows in the south wall are in contrast to plain coloured glass on the south.

Outside, the well kept churchyard is still used for funerals. One interesting gravestone records the long service to the church of Captain R. (Richard) C. Hall, MC, who was churchwarden from 1928 and served the church for 60 years. The present churchwarden has been in post for some time, so there have only been two churchwardens in the present century. The altar is of simple wooden construction.

The Wesleyan Chapel, several hundred metres from the church, and close to the village pub, predates the church, and was erected in 1837. No longer used, it has been turned into a house.

In Loving Memory
of
JOHN ALFRED WARNER
WHO DIED JULY 1st 1916.
AGED 42 YEARS.
"JESUS CALLED A LITTLE
CHILD UNTO HIM"

flore
church of all saints

Each church is sited in its own unique place, and at Flore, the Church of All Saints is set to the south-west of the village. Here it shares the area with other ancient buildings, including Flore House and the Mill. Nearby are more recent buildings, including the Church of England Primary School, and the old Tithe House – now called The Old Manor. The Old Vicarage is beyond Flore House, and there were problems in the 1830s when the Vicar claimed a right of way across the grounds that belonged the squire. The problem is no longer relevant because the incumbent lives at Nether Heyford – Flore lost its vicar in 1996 and is now part of the benefice of four parishes.

The church is almost cocooned amongst superb old trees, of which a blue cedar, close to the chancel wall, is the most prominent. There are several hundred headstones and tombs, the oldest of which is now mounted in the west wall of the churchyard, and this predates the church registers that begin in 1853. Beyond the churchyard there are some superb views across the surrounding countryside, with the still relatively infant Nene almost within a stone's throw of the church – beyond that the Roman Watling Street, now the A5, is visible, and certainly within earshot! Two long distance footpaths, The Nene Way and the MacMillan Way, pass through the churchyard, and walkers often rest on the seats to admire the panoramic view.

The church is a Grade II* Listed Building, and two tombs that stand near the south door are separately listed. The church is built from a mellow brown sandstone which for more than 700 years has, not surprisingly, suffered greatly from the weather. The embattled west tower has four bell openings and it, together with the nave, is in Early English style, owing its existence to early 13th century craftsmen. The tower has a ring of six bells, together with a priest's bell. The earliest of these was cast in 1676, followed by a further three in 1679, with two more following in 1743. The ring of bells was increased from five in 1700. The inscription on the pres-

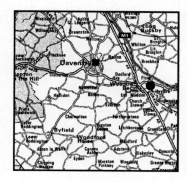

ent tenor bell, which bears the date 1743, replaces what is perhaps a more interesting inscription recorded in 1700, which said "Be it known to all that do mee see that Bagley of Chacom made mee in 1679". Having had little use since the 1930s, because of the unsafe nature of the framework, the bells were taken down in 1957. Retuning and rehanging was possible after the first of Flore's successful Flower Festivals, held in 1963. The 'new' bells were rung for the first time at Easter 1964.

The south doorway is reached through a porch that still has the original oaken doors and stone seats, added to the church in 1500. The south door dates from around 1200, and the arch, with its detailed zigzag decorations, could perhaps be considered almost flamboyant. Perhaps surprisingly, the modern door has what is perhaps a unique feature – a cat flap was installed and used by Whiskey, the resident feline, though he died many years ago. Interesting carved faces are features of the porch, and that above the arch is in good condition, though the three around the original doorway have suffered from erosion.

Inside the church, both north and south aisles embrace the west tower. This often happened when additions were made to churches to protect the original tower. Three fine arches gives access into the vestry, tower and kitchen from the nave. 13th century piers and arches separate the nave from the aisle, and each pier has a central pillar around which is a cluster of three small shafts, culminating in superb examples of double chamfered arches. Leaf capitals have been carved on one of the piers and its responds. The columns in the south aisle have been carved from a different material to that used in the north aisle, which suggests they are of a slightly different date. The windows, in Decorated style, have net tracery, and are probably also 14th century in origin.

About 1852 the Rev. Kenneth Tarpley made dramatic changes to the nave of All Saints Church when he bricked up three arches and inserted an iron gallery at the back of the nave for the use of singers. At the same time he also removed the roof, lowered it, and inserted a new ceiling with a small dome. Clerestory windows were also put in at this time. The earlier roof line is still visible on the side of the tower. During this work, the old oak pews were removed from the church, and replaced with high-backed deal seating. Certain pews were also allocated to various houses in the parish at this time.

The following two incumbents were obviously not impressed with the work which the Rev. Tarpley had done, and all of it, with the exception of the ceiling and clerestory, was taken out by the Rev. F. P. Johnson and the Rev. William Norris between 1870 and 1880. The Rev. Norris was also responsible for lowering the floor of the nave by 16 inches (40 cm) to enable the bases of the columns to be seen. The pews that had been in the church for just over thirty years were also replaced.

When Mrs Pack of Flore House donated a new font in 1832, the Rev. Tarpley removed the Saxon font, which found a new use as a cattle trough in a field off Spout Lane. Here it rested for some time before being spotted by the Vicar of Dodford, who arranged for it to be taken into his church. When the Rev. Johnson arrived in 1865, the font was offered back to the Church of All Saints, and the ancient stone was returned to Flore. The font was re-sited in 1966 to its present position just inside the south door, and sits on a base made from a millstone from Towcester Mill, a large grindstone from Northampton and a small grindstone from the wheelwright's yard in Flore.

At the end of the two aisles there are stained glass windows to the memory of those killed in the 1914–18 war. The window in the north aisle is dedicated to all the men of Flore, and is brightly coloured. The inscription in the upper lights of this window reads *UBIQUE QUO FAS DUCUNT ET GLORIA*, around which is a cannon and a crown. Below can be seen the crest of the Northamptonshire Regiment, and the words *Hindoo Stan and XVIII Leicestershire*. In the lower lights are three figures. On the left, regaled with armour and holding a sword and shield, is the Archangel St. Michael, with the inscription *QUIS ET DEUS*. The central figure is that of Our Lord, holding a crown of gold in his hand. On the right is a portrait of a young St. George standing guard over a dragon that he has slain. The inscription reads *Be Thou Faithful Unto Death and I will Give you a Crown of Life*.

The window at the east end of the south aisle commemorates Lt Bruce Lorence Capell, MC. Lt Capell was killed at Arras in 1918, and is buried in Bellacourt Military Cemetery, Riviere. The wooden cross originally mounted on his grave is now on the wall adjacent to the window. The memorial included the citation for his bravery, and records that he fell in Andinfer. Near to this window in the south east corner of the nave there was formerly a

> *The window was designed and provided by his father, Bruce Capell, an architect who practised in London, but who owned a house and land in Flore. In addition to this window Bruce Capell also designed the village War Memorial on High Street on the A45, which was said to be modelled on the Queen Eleanor Cross at Geddington.*

lady altar, served by a piscina that can still be seen in the wall. This piscina, which has an attractive ogee arch with cusps and fleurons surmounting it, is based on a design brought back by the Crusaders.

The nave is divided from the chancel by a 15th century rood screen in oak, with doors opening into the chancel. There would have been a rood loft above the screen reached by stairways in the walls on either side, so that lights could be placed near the rood. The stair on the north side was opened up in 1907, but that on the south behind the pulpit remains closed. Close to the stairway in the front of the nave there is a stone marked with a cross, placed here in 1907. The stone was discovered when the chancel floor was lowered in 1840, and placed outside the Priest's Door on the south wall. Daniel Robinson (1828–1909), sexton and clerk of the Parochial Church Council for 42 years, wrote a detailed history of the church. He claimed that this was a 'Gospel Stone', and had originally been erected on a mound as a centre for worship before there was a church building. When the stone was re-located to the nave in 1907, Major C. A. Markham, author of *Stone Crosses of Northamptonshire* (1900), concluded that the stone was in fact a 12th or 13th century coffin lid. The Rural Dean, who said he had a similar stone in his church, supported Markham's observations, but opinion is still divided.

At the rear of the nave, the centre arch contains a 'Hilditch Screen', which came with the organ in 1861 and remained at the back of the church when the organ was moved to the chancel in 1899. Also at the rear of the church, near the south door, is a copy of Sandro Boticelli's 'The Madonna of the Rosebush', given by Mrs Lodge in memory of her late husband, Francis Brodie Lodge, of Flore House.

In addition to the four carvings in the porch, there are three more faces inside the church. One particularly ugly creation is in the ground floor of the tower. The others are green men peering out from the foliage in the capitals of two of the columns in the north aisle. The chancel is at a slight angle to the nave, because it was built after the nave.

> *This arrangement is an example of a 'weeping chancel', because it weeps away from the line of the nave.*

The double piscina which serves the altar is on the south wall, and is of the Early English period, but is no longer is use. The outlet has been blocked and the front of the bowl, which projected into the sanctuary, has been broken off. There is a single sedilia adjacent to this, a seat for the priest, who would retire here for those parts of the service in which he was not involved.

On the north wall of the sanctuary is the aumbry, made by Danis Dauksta in 1980, where the sacramental Body and Blood of Christ is kept. Formerly this was the Easter Sepulchre where, during the Middle Ages, the sacrament and crucifix were placed on Good Friday, where they stayed until communion on Easter Day. Above the aumbry window there is Romanesque (Norman) carving in the stone that is mounted in the sill. It is possible that this may have been preserved from an earlier church. The stained glass in the east window was installed in 1903 to commemorate Queen Victoria's jubilee, and was paid for by subscription The organ, restored, enlarged and moved to the chancel in 1899, is now virtually obsolete, having been replaced by an electronic organ in the front of the north aisle in 1997. The original vestry is situated behind the old pipe organ, and earlier county historians recorded that a memorial to Robert Saunders (1569) stood here. However, this is no longer is position and its whereabouts is not known. The room is currently used as a store.

There are three ancient brasses in the chancel floor, but a protective carpet now covers them. Historian John Bridges, whose survey of Flore was in September 1719, described these brasses in detail in his history of the county. The oldest is to Thomas Knaresburgh and his wife – he died in 1450 and she in 1488. Their brasses include two 23 in (57 cm) figures. The second brass, dated 1510, commemorates Henry Mitchell and his wife Phillipa. The third is to the memory of Alyce Wryley, who died in 1537, but the memorial has been damaged, and only the foot of the cross that formed the central part of the brass now remains.

> *During his refurbishment of the church, the Rev. K. M. R. Tarpley re-sited the brasses, and in the process assembled them incorrectly.*

Most of the other memorials in the floor of the chancel are to families who lived in Flore House. Both Bridges and Baker record others, but several of the large stone slabs that were formerly in the chancel can now be found at the back of the church, their places in the chancel having been taken by 19th centuries worthies.

The Enyon family, who built Flore House in 1612, are still commemorated in several memorials. James Enyon was killed in a duel while in the Royalist army at Gloucester in 1642. His infant son was buried in Flore, with a similar small black marble slab to that of his nephew Sidney Stanley, who died in 1652 when less than a month old. Sir James' widow, Dorothy, remarried, and is commemorated as Dorothy Wryley on a large stone, which that records that she died in 1678 at the age of 83.

One the south side of the chancel is the Priest's door, now rarely used, but which formerly enabled the vicar to enter the church and reach the vestry, then the north side of the chancel, without having to go through the crowded porch. On the outside of the doorway some heavy 13th century dogtooth decoration still survives. The chancel was re-roofed in the 1870s, leaving dark woodwork in the inside, and in 1963 the Rev. Richard Yates commissioned architect Dykes Bower to produce decorated ceiling panels. Once installed the chancel immediately became much lighter. At the same time, Mr Brodie Lodge provided new fittings in the chancel and a 15th century Italian marble bas relief of the Virgin Child, which was mounted on the south wall.

As with almost all churches, All Saints has been in frequent need of repair, and with the many changes in worship patterns over the centuries alterations have been necessary to improve facilities. The most recent work was carried out early in 1999, when pews were removed from both the front and rear of the nave and a new nave altar was provided. These has provided more space to allow people to congregate, and with the addition of new carpets, gives the church a more inviting appearance. These repairs and renovations are possible because of the hugely successful annual Flore Flower Festival and Open Gardens, that bring in a substantial sum of money each summer. Hundreds of visitors pass through the church to admire the floral arrangements.

The maintenance of the chancel was the responsibility of Christ Church, Oxford, the patron of the living. In the 19th century the chancel fell into disrepair and the Bishop had to negotiate finance to allow the major repairs of the 1870s. In 1881 Christ Church sold the former Tithe House and an area of pasture, and the responsibility for the chancel fell to the purchaser. In recent years, the owners of the house and land have paid a cash sum to release them from further liability, and this is invested in a trust fund for future chancel repairs.

great brington
church of st andrew

The fact that the Church of St. Andrew houses the chapel of the Spencers of Althorp has long been of interest to both historians and lay people, but this interest increased during the marriage, and later the death, of Diana, Princess of Wales, the daughter of one of the Earls of Spencer. As everyone knows, Diana met her untimely death in the now infamous car crash in a Parisian tunnel.

The church tower stands – some would say – like a lofty beacon over the surrounding countryside, including the Althorp estate, and it is here within their own private chapel that innumerable members of the Spencer family are buried.

The church is approached from either the west or east, through gate piers, from which hang the superbly crafted iron gates, erected in 1840, and relatively recent additions when compared to the rest of the church. Entrance is via the south doorway, with its attractive internal glass doors.

The large and well-proportioned building, built of Northamptonshire ironstone, has an elegant 13th century west tower. The bell openings consist of two lancets under a single arch. The tower houses a ring of seven bells, including a priest's bell, and with the exception of the priest's bell, they all bear inscriptions, but not all have dates. However, three are marked 1723. Interestingly, the priest's bell purportedly once hung in nearby Holdenby House. Tradition suggests that it was known as King Charles' Dinner Bell, and when he was imprisoned at Holdenby it was used to call him to meals. At one time, it is said, there was an inscription that read "King Charles it is said, I speak from the Heavens".

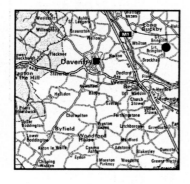

The west doorway is from the Perpendicular period, and there is a large west window. The nave, consisting of two six-bay arcades, features Decorated arches that contrast with the north aisle. Here the lower arches are double chamfered, and rest on octagonal piers and responds. In the south aisle, similar tall slender octagonal piers can be found, again with responds. When the chancel was rebuilt, the cost was borne by Sir John Spencer. Records from the 17th century make reference to an inscription in the chancel windows, which confirm that John Spencer carried out the re-building work. It was the intention to make the north chapel the family chapel.

It is thought that the north aisle may have been due to the efforts of Sir William Spencer, because a window bearing the date 1526 referred to him. The south doorway dates from about 1300, and close to it in the same south wall there is a gabled outer tomb recess carved with dogtooth decoration, suggesting that it dates from about the same time as the doorway. Edward Blore, who also worked for William IV, Queen Victoria and Westminster Abbey, replaced the south porch in 1832.

The flat blank pointed arches on the circular font carved from Purbeck marble have panels decorated with crosses and flowers. The font stands on a 13th century stone base, and is embellished with dogtooth markings. The makers of the benches, although from 1846 being of relatively recent vintage, have incorporated pieces from much older 15th century furniture, and all exhibit traditional poppy heads – ornamental finials carved on the ends of benches, and which first appeared in churches in the 15th century. Most of them take the form of the fleur-de-lis. The bench at the west end of the north side clearly shows carved hands in an extended, reaching out, pose. Some of the other furniture dates from the 17th century, and includes a poor box on a shaped coarse column, and the communion rail. The south door also dates from this period, and is probably an original.

The stained glass in the chancel south window is medieval, and owes its existence to a bequest in the will of Sir William Spencer, who died in 1532. It includes the figure of St. John the Baptist, together with other emblems, including a woman praying, some small saintly figures, a lamb and a man blowing a horn. The exquisite east window is of a much later date, and was placed in the church by the sixth Earl to commemorate the life of the fifth Earl. The work was carried out by William Morris of Morris and Co in 1912, and shows the Adoration of the Lamb.

Monuments in the chancel include a brass with a half figure of a priest, to John de Clipston who died in 1344. Another memorial takes the form of a tombstone with a shield relief to Laurence Washington, buried in 1616. The arms of the Washington family can be seen on the stone, and consist of three red stars and stripes with a white shield. The inscription shows that this is the last resting place of Laurence Washington and his wife.

The original iron railings that surround the Spencer monuments prevent people from entering. It is here, in this family-controlled part of the church, that one of the most intriguing and – according to some historians – the most complete set of monuments of any family in the country still exists virtually intact.

At one time there was a stairway towards the east end of the south aisle, but this has been blocked off. Such a feature would have given access to the rood loft. The roofs in both the chancel and nave still retain some of their ancient beams. The richly carved reredos is modern, and is fronted by a 17th century communion rail with rather hefty looking balusters (the pillars along the length of the

balustrade which support the rails).

Rebuilding of the chancel and the exterior of north chapel took place in 1846, and was carried out by the architect Edward Blore (see earlier). The idea for the design of the bay window in the north wall of the chapel, with its intricate fan vaulting, came from Henry VII's chapel in Westminster. The stained glass in the chapel window was put there by Ward, and the chapel, with three bays, still has its original stained glass by Ward, who had advice from Charles Winston, the acknowledged expert of the period.

The idea for a Spencer family chapel came from Sir John Spencer, who died in 1522. It is he who added the north chapel to the present building with the express purpose of using it as the resting place for members of his immediate family, and for future generations of Spencers. It has been suggested that Thomas Heritage, who was Rector of Great Brington at the time, was responsible for the design. Thomas Heritage later went on to become Surveyor of the King's Works. That he designed the chapel at Great Brington cannot be proven, as he was only appointed to the position of Surveyor of the King's Work in about 1530, seventeen years after the chapel was built.

A rearrangement of the Spencer monuments has taken place in the chapel, with the exception of those sited between the chapel and chancel. Latterly the Spencers have insisted that the chapel is locked, and the original iron railings that surround that part of the building prevent people from entering. It is here, in this family-controlled part of the church, that one of the most intriguing and, according to some historians, the most complete set of monuments of any family in the country still exists virtually intact.

Perhaps not surprisingly the oldest monument is to Sir John Spencer, the instigator of the project who died in 1522, and his wife. The effigies of these two lie prone on a tall tomb chest, she with two small puppy sculptures at her feet. The tomb is positioned beneath a canopy, on the inside of which is a wide panelled arch with four centres. Just beneath the apex of the canopy is a delightful figure of an angel.

Sir William Spencer died in 1532, and although the effigies are no longer on the tomb chest, this part of the memorial – together with an inscription tablet– still remains below the east window. The Sir John

Spencer who died in 1586 rests with his wife. The memorial is by Jasper Hollemans from Burton-on-Trent, and takes the form of a tall tomb chest upon which rest the two recumbent figures. Lady Spencer is complete with an extremely weighty hood. The tomb is adorned with much embellishment and shields, separated by strips with rudimentary details.

The memorial to Robert, first Baron Spencer, and his wife are situated to the west of that of the 1586 tomb of Sir John Spencer. This is also the work of Hollemans, and it was put in place in 1599. Both figures recline on a strapwork painted sarcophagus. Robert wears armour, and his wife is dressed in an even larger hood than that worn by the wife of Sir John. Over the lower half of her body the sculptor has placed a coverlet, with heraldic symbols. This is an unusual, some historians suggest, unique feature to be found on a tomb.

Jasper Hollemans is again responsible for the monument that now stands against the wall in the north-east corner. This is the tallest of the monuments in the chapel, and prior to 1846 it was a free-standing memorial. This is to the Sir John Spencer, who died in 1599, and who is accompanied by his wife.

When Nicholas Stone produced the memorial for William Lord Spencer, who died in 1636, he was paid £600, and of this £14 was handed over to John Hargrave, who carved the effigy of the Lord, and £15 was given to Richard White for the effigy of the Lady. This is a striking detached eight-poster monument, whose black marble columns are crowned by white marble capitals. Small arches along the sides connect these columns. The tomb chest, also carved from black and white marble, supports the white effigies that lie on a black moulded lid.

The memorial for Sir Edward Spencer is in the south-west corner. The monument was erected in 1656, one year after his death, and is the work of John Stone. This memorial is markedly different to the previous memorials, in that it has a demi-figure rising from the Urn of the Resurrection. The square pillar of the Word of God is to his right, with the Column of Truth on the left, on which rests a Bible. Joseph Nollekens, who produced busts of all the important people of his day, was responsible for the large hanging monument to John, Earl Spencer (1783). In this a female figure stands on clouds where she supports a medallion bearing a profile of the Earl, who is also on clouds. At her feet there is a large cornucopia – a horn of plenty – overflowing with flowers, fruit and corn. The poem that accompanies the monument is worth reading.

John Flaxman was responsible for the monument, placed on the west wall, to Georgiana Countess of Spencer, who died in 1814. This was originally designed to be a base for the Nollekens memorial to John, Earl Spencer, and is of an extremely simple design, featuring an oblong table that carries an inscription in the middle. To the left can be seen faith, and to the right what has been described as a "noble and loveable figure of charity". Flaxman was responsible for statues in Westminster Abbey, including that of Burns, and he also completed friezes at Buckingham Palace. Collections of his drawings can be seen in a number of galleries, the British Museum and University College, London.

Interestingly, the priest's bell purportedly once hung in nearby Holdenby House. Tradition suggests that it was known as King Charles' Dinner Bell, and when he was imprisoned at Holdenby it was used to call him to meals. At one time, it is said, there was an inscription that read "King Charles it is said, I speak from the Heavens".

The monument to Captain Robert Cavendish Spencer by Chantrey is to the east of the bay window. This is less elaborate than some of the other memorials, and consists of a bust on a plinth. In addition to these easily recognisable monuments, there are many small ones, including coffin plates that have been sunk into the floor of the bay window. To complement the monuments and memorials a variety of cornets, helmets, gauntlets, swords and hatchments are also in evidence.

Outside in the churchyard there is an interesting churchyard cross, which has been carved to produce a concave-sided shaft.

hellidon
church of st john the baptist

Hellidon is a delightful small Northamptonshire village which retains all its rural charm. The church, hidden from the lower levels, stands on a high point on the edge of the settlement. Although parts of the present church have stood on the site for more than six hundred years, it is likely there was at least one previous church building – the records for the earliest go back to the 12th century, showing that towards the end of the 12th century there was a chapel "in the parish of Catesby". When Bridges *History of Northamptonshire* was was published, Catesby (with its one-time priory) was the mother church of Staverton. With the reorganisation of parishes in 1953, Hellidon, Staverton and Catesby came together as a united benefice, with one Rector serving all three villages.

The church can be reached from the village either up the narrow lane nearly opposite the phone box, or via the steps to the right at the entrance to the same lane. Entry is gained via the south doorway, through the south porch, on the left of which there are steep grooves in the stonework. Legend has it that these were carved by soldiers who sharpened their swords on the way to the Battle of Edgehill in late 1642. Equally, it is possible that local farm labourers may have ground their scythes here. The 1591 date stone over the south door suggests that the porch was also built at the same time as the main church.

The tower, complete with buttresses and battlements, is the earliest part of the building, having been constructed in 1350, and even a cursory glance will show the different building styles and material. At one time the tower was adorned with four pinnacles, but these were removed in 1847. The tower contains a ring of four bells, one of which bears an inscription and the date 1615; the other three are engraved with various inscriptions and the date 1635. Originally cast by Hugh Watts at his bellfoundry in Leicester, they were removed from the bell chamber in 1960 and rehung with a new frame. Further work was carried out in 1993 at the Whitechapel bellfoundry. When the bells were rehung a fifth was added.

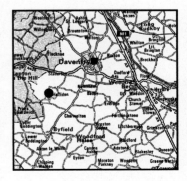

67

Inside the building, little earlier craftsmanship remains. Hellidon's church was in such a bad state of repair that it was necessary to almost raze it to the ground during the 19th century, when it was the norm to 'modernise' these old buildings. Much restoration work took place when the Rev. Charles Holthouse was Vicar, with his friend the architect William Butterfield being called in to do the work. According to a report in 1845, the chancel floor had holes in it and the pews were dilapidated. The walls of the building were taken down to a few feet above ground level, and the nave and chancel were rebuilt in 1847. This restoration work cost a total of £800. Further work took place over the next fifty years, with additions including the north aisle (1867), which is made up of three bays. The vestry was completed in 1897, to commemorate Queen Victoria's Diamond Jubilee.

By far the most poignant memorial is to an 11 year old lad. Levi Watkins had saved a younger boy who had fallen into the village well. Having brought the youngster safely to the surface, the eager onlookers pulled him to safety, forgetting about Levi who fell back into the water and was drowned.

There are a number of interesting stained glass windows in the building. That to the east of the south door shows four soldiers, commemorated for laying down their lives during the 1914–18 war. Although the men wear an earlier form of battledress – suits of shining armour – their faces were taken from photographs, and are reputed to be good likenesses, making this particular memorial unique. The stained glass in the large east window in the chancel was produced at a cost of £55.15s (£55.75p), and is showing serious signs of wear, with some of the glass bowing. Even though the window is attractive from a distance, with its range of coloured glass, the images are not particularly well crafted. However, there is attractive stained glass west window in the tower that shows the figure of St. John the Baptist, the church's patron saint.

Two further windows in the chancel are in memory of Fanny Lee, who died in 1876. When the Rev. Charles Holthouse arrived in Hellidon, he had to purchase a property to live in. He also quickly established a preparatory school for boys, for which Fanny Lee acted as matron. The window arches, with their polychrome features, are a trademark of William Butterfield, who was also responsible for the decorations on the ceiling beams, features common to many of the churches with which he was involved.

The present two-manual organ, now in the chancel, was originally in the north aisle. Built by a Mr Pease in London 1896, it cost £150, and was moved into its present position when this part of the church was added in 1897. Prior to this, music was provided by a Chappell harmonium, installed in 1867. It costs were met by subscription from past pupils, masters and parents of the local preparatory school.

The churchyard is worth a look, interesting features including the memorial to the Rev. Charles Scrofton Holthouse, which takes the form of the tall monument at the front of the churchyard as you approach the building from the west end. There is a metal gravestone behind the tower, towards the south and back of the churchyard.

litchborough
church of st martin

This village has a variety of stone buildings which, together with the Hall, give the place its unique character. It was first recorded in the Domesday Survey, when it was known as 'Liceberge'. The church, situated in a pleasant area of the village, with small areas of green close to the gate, and with the fallen remembered by the war memorial close by, continues to serve the parishioners of this small village as it has done for centuries past.

The simply-fashioned, buttressed west tower is rounded off with battlements. The tower holds a ring of five bells, which bear various dates. The oldest is from 1628, followed by one from 1753, recast in 1922. The 1878 bell only hung in the tower a few years before it was recast in 1895. John Taylor and Co. of Loughborough cast the two other bells in the early part of this century (1902 and 1909). The plain west door originally led into the ringing chamber, but is no longer used.

The short walk to the south porch is along a well maintained path, and just inside the gate an ancient conifer spreads itself across a large area of the churchyard. Once inside the south porch, the fascinating information about the once-lapsed churchyard project gives details of the revised plan for the work (a sheet inside the church also shows the recent assessor's report!). Access to the church is through the south doorway, with this and its opposite north doorway being from the Decorated period. Inside the porch the list of rectors makes interesting reading. The first, High de Edward, was appointed in 1209, but no services were held in any churches in England during the period 1208–1213 as King John was in dispute with Rome and England lay under the Pope. Further perusal of the list shows the possible effects of the Black, which started in 1348 during Edward III's reign. John de Aylesbury was appointed in May 1349, John Mallore in August and John le Clerc in December.

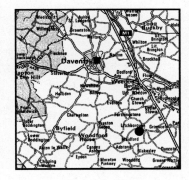

Unlike many churches, most of the Church of St. Martin of Tours can be attributed to one building phase, the Decorated period. Started in the 12th century, it is likely it was the successor of an earlier church that probably stood on the same site. Some historians also believe that only part of the church was completed, and that a north aisle was to have been included. It is likely that the church was attacked during the Civil war, and it has been suggested that Cromwell's soldiers were responsible for destroying a great deal of St Martin's ancient glass.

In the early part of the 19th century a gallery had been placed at the west end of the church. When William Browning was Rector, he provided a great deal of money for renovations. One of the things he did was to remove the gallery which, according to contemporary reports, was considered ugly. During this work the old pews were taken out and a new roof put over the chancel. In addition, Browning was responsible for opening up two leper windows, which he then filled with stained glass. Work also took place to elevate sanctuary. The space between the church and tower was also opened, and at the same time a stained glass window showing the Church's patron saint was placed there.

Entering St. Martin's Church is a wonderful experience. There is a feeling of light and life, and the variety of materials on display, including work by children, gives the building a feeling of being used and cared for. The nave has a south arcade made up of four bays, with double chamfered arches supported by octagonal piers. The nave's clerestory has quatrefoil windows, and these allow extra light into the building. Interesting figures keep guard as they gaze down from both sides of the bases of the arches.

One of the delights of St. Martin's Church is the stained glass. There are many interesting examples of the craftsman's art, and one of the pleasing features is that for each window there is a written card. The visitor is thus given a greater understanding of the story behind

STAINED GLASS RESTORATION

The restoration process is called 'isothermal glazing'. This allows air inside the church to pass evenly over both surfaces of the glass, which ensures that the temperature on both the internal and external surfaces remains the same – thus, condensation no longer forms. The glass is removed to be cleaned. The dirty glass is swabbed with deionsed water, which removes any loose material. The edges of the pieces that are damaged, together with any that has been repaired before, will be bonded with silicone adhesive. Any missing pieces, or those that are beyond repair, will be replaced by pieces of glass which have been hand-painted to ensure that colour match and texture is as accurate as possible. Once this process is completed, all the glass is put into manganese bronze frames and covered with protective glazing. When the windows are re-installed they will have a form of double glazing, which means that the old glass will be separated from the external air, but at the same time both surfaces will be ventilated.

each window. In the south aisle westerly window – to the left of the door – the left-hand side of the window is based on St. Luke Chapter 23 v 53; the right-hand side on St. Matthew Chapter 28 v 4, and these were installed in memory of William and Arthur Grant. Two windows in the north wall contain remnants of medieval stained glass dating from between 1320 and 1340. The illustrations show the Annunciation and a Trinity shield. Nearby can be seen the Archangel Gabriel holding a scroll, and Mary with a vase of lilies.

Over the years this early glass has become badly corroded, inside and out. The glass has collected an external layer that is supporting a variety of organic growth, which is causing damage. As a result, the features on the internal face of the glass have become almost totally obliterated. Repairs which have been carried out in the past, and which have led to a great deal of the detail being hidden, have exacerbated the problems.

To decide on the best course of action, advice was sought from conservation experts, who suggested ways of arresting the decline in the quality of the windows. To help raise the funds, a Millennium Project has been set up, and once enough money is raised, the renovatory work will be carried out. The cleaning and preservation is costly because it needs careful expert attention, and professionals are being used for the work. Once the process has been completed, not only will any further damage be reduced, but the colour of the windows will also be improved. The process that is to be used at Litchborough is called 'isothermal glazing' (see above). This technique has already been used successfully in the sanctuary's south window, where the rare yellow sundial was subjected to the same process.

The window in the chancel has three traceries, and originally the central roundels had heads that featured crowns, and behind was a range of foliage. Although the heads have gone, the crowns and foliage still remain, but the effect of corrosion has caused deep pitting of the glass's surface. When pieces of the original glass were lost, the missing segments were infilled with clear glass. The ancient glass that remains was crafted more than 650 years ago, and is of great historical interest. Of the other windows, those on the north and south of the chancel have reticulated tracery of the Decorated period. The east window is from the Perpendicular period, and the five lower lights of this window in the chancel show various scenes from the life of Jesus. Here too, is a piscina in the south wall – its use has been superseded by more modern disposal methods, so it has found a new use as a flower vase.

The large tomb chest on the north of the chancel next to the pulpit was erected in 1633 in memory of Sir John Ne(e)dham. Sir John inhabited the Manor, to the south of the church, until it was deviated by fire. Litchborough Hall, on the Banbury Road, replaced it in the 17th/18th centuries. The alabaster effigy of Sir John is a fine example of its kind, and information about the deceased can be seen on a tablet let into the wall behind. According to the Victoria County History, at the time at which it was placed in the church it exhibited the latest 'military pillow' in Northamptonshire. The inscription on the tomb tells us that Needham was "gentleman pensioner unto the late Queene Elizabeth of Happie Memorie and afterward unto our late soveraigne, Lord King James; and was by them both well esteemed, and likewise by the noble persons of the best ranke and qualitie".

The Church contains a number of memorials to the Grant family. Of Scottish origin, they moved south and occupied the Hall from 1740 until 1971. The south aisle contains a memorial to Frances Simpson Grant, who died in 1907, and takes the form of a white marble angel, with outstretched arms. Other interesting points include the rector's pew, the plain tub font, whose restoration history is recorded on the plinth, and the hatchments which hang in the church and vestry.

Outside, enjoy the churchyard with its regular wildlife visitors. Because many churchyards consist of unimproved grassland, they are valuable as wildlife sites. The churchyard, like several others in the county, has a conservation policy, which in 1980 earned it a coveted award. The map and information in the south porch explains how the area is managed as a wildlife habitat. Some twenty species of plants and ferns have been recorded on the church wall itself. Francesca Greenoak's gives special mention to St. Martin's churchyard in her book *God's Acre*, which deals with churchyard conservation. In 1985 the author indicated that the drystone wall, which marks the boundary of Litchborough's churchyard, was the most easterly point at which navelwort or wall pennywort had been recorded. It is also interesting that under the terms of an ancient tradition, the Rector has the right to graze six sheep and four goats in the churchyard! On the south wall, remains of an earlier scratch dial can be seen. Walk around to the north doorway to peer at an interesting gargoyle, which in turn stares back unmovingly, even disapprovingly!

One especially poignant tombstone in the churchyard is for a Royalist soldier, his small, simple tombstone now close to the path to the north of the tower. How he came to end up in Litchborough will probably always remain a mystery, though it is probable that he escaped from Naseby and made his way to the village.

long buckby
church of st lawrence

In spite of the relatively rapid growth of Long Buckby, the Church of St Lawrence still stands on the edge of the village, with rolling countryside touching its boundary. The village has a long history, and was recorded as Beckebi in the *Domesday Book* (1086). No one is certain when the first church appeared, but a number of references before the Reformation (16th century) mention a Chapel of our Lady in the Parish of St Gregory, and this included a variety of bequests. Considered to be a 'chantry chapel', this was resolved by the Bishop of Peterborough in 1545, who informed the parishioners that no such chapel existed – a great relief as it meant they did not have to make contributions to it and its upkeep.

The tower is the earliest part of the present church, and either dates from the late 12th or early 13th century. If of the earlier date it is transitional Norman rather than Early English. Its battlements, and the gargoyles, were added at a later date, and it has interesting architectural work just below these. Some authorities suggest that the tower may have been rendered when it was built. Whereas this is impossible to prove, it was certainly plastered over during Victorian times, when it is recorded in 1883 that "the coating of plaster that disfigured the Early English tower has been removed". However, only three sides of the tower were dealt with, the fourth (west) side being completed during work in 1886.

A drawing of the church in about 1840 shows that the tower roof was much higher than it is now, and took the form of a pyramid. The lowering of this took place in Victorian times. At some point in the past, the tower was enhanced with four short, rather stout pinnacles. The bell openings are of the two-light kind, separated by a restored shaft. There is some evidence that at one time there was a door on the west side of the tower, possibly the original entrance to the church. However, it has been impossible to determine where such a west door would have been, as there does not appear to be any evidence inside the church.

A further look at the tower shows it is embraced by the nave, which suggests that later craftsmen did not

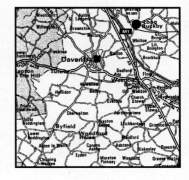

want to disturb the original tower when extensions were being made. The tower contains three bells which are thought to have been cast in Hugh Watt's Leicester bellfoundry in 1624, though there is some doubt about the fifth. The number one bell was recast in 1814, and all the bells were taken down in 1899, the first time they had left the tower for almost 300 years. According to the churchwarden, writing in November 1897, "The five bells of the Church are reported by Messrs Taylor and Sons to be in an unsatisfactory and unsafe condition, owing to the decay of the frames in which they are hung and of the beams which support them". Having been removed, together with the accompanying framework, they were rehung and retuned, and new steel beams replaced the original wooden structures. The work took some eight weeks to complete. They were again rehung by the same bellfoundry in 1950.

> As Long Buckby has a long history of being without a Lord of the Manor, there is marked a lack of memorials in the church. However, there is an interesting one in the north aisle, to 12 year old Cilena Bradley, who died in 1726. Another interesting monument is to Elizabeth Clerk, and it is recorded on her stone that she died instantaneously as a result of being frightened when four drunks broke into the house.

One of the interesting features of St. Lawrence's Church, like so many, is the improvement in the building work. Mostly formed from ironstone, the virtually random masonry of the tower gives way to the more carefully carved blocks of the clerestory of the nave and the chancel. Further changes occur where ashlar has been used for the north and south aisles. A look up towards the roof of the building shows the obvious roof line that can be seen on the east wall of the nave above the chancel.

A further tour of the outside of the building shows that a round headed door, originating during the Georgian restoration of 1774, can be seen in the east wall of the south aisle. It is possible that the triangular commemorative stone, now below the second window from the west on the north wall, and dated 1774, may at one time have been above the now blocked in doorway. The rest of the building dates mainly from the 14th century, and is in Decorated style.

The church is reached along a pathway lined by pollarded limes, an attractive feature found around all the paths in the churchyard, adding to the atmosphere. The south porch was restored in 1883, but the remains of a once-carved figure can still be seen. The triple chamfered tower arch was originally open, and the infilling took place late in 1959, a local architect carrying out the work. The ringing floor is no longer at ground level.

The nave consists of arcades made up of four bays and originating during the Decorated period. The octagonal piers have double chamfered arches. In the south aisle there are three corbels – these are stone brackets, but they were often carved with heads on them. The most westerly of the three has either a blacksmith or cobbler's head, the next one represents a female wearing the typical square headdress reminiscent of Edward II's (1327–1377) reign, and three fleur-de-lis arranged as a coronet. The third of the corbels takes the form of a crowned head.

roof has been replaced since the church was built – the previous nave was too low to support a clerestory, so it was raised during the work car-

ried out by G. G. Scott in 1862, the first of the Victorian restorative pro-
grammes. The windows consist of foiled circles arranged in pairs. The earlier pews were also taken out at this time, and new ones, designed by
Scott, replaced them. It was also during this 1862 work that the galleries,
erected in Georgian times, were removed.

The pulpit is a piece of modern craftsmanship, and given to the church
in 1955 in memory not only of John Joseph Haynes and his wife Annie
Elizabeth, but also as a mark of appreciation for the work which the
Sunday School teachers who worked with them did.

The chancel is in Decorated style, although this area has been renovated and the windows altered. The east window is dedicated to the wife
of a former Vicar, the daughter of the Rev. G. L. Yate, and was probably
installed during the restorative work in 1862. The windows show the arms
of the Yate family – showing three gates, which is unique – and the See of
Peterborough. The window depicts three bible stories: the Good
Shepherd, Annunciation and Resurrection.

The sanctuary has the usual piscina (on the south side) which was used
for cleaning the communion vessels. This is in Decorated style, as are the
three seats of the sedilia that would have been for the priest and deacons.
The ogee arches are considered crude, and the simple hood moulds may
have been restored at some time. On the north end of the east wall there
is a pedestal that probably had a niche in which stood a statue of St.
Lawrence, the church's patron saint. The Rev. Aubrey Leake, who lived in
Long Buckby as a youngster, gave the present statue. The east end of the
north aisle is the site of a former Lady Chapel, information about its existence having being gleaned from earlier wills.

Langton Freeman, the Lord of the Manor in the 18th century,
gave a sum of £400 on deposit, the interest from which was to
be used to teach the poor of the parish to read,
write and 'cast accounts', as well a being
able to recite the catechism.
School cost 1d a
week for those who
could afford it. It
was free for the rest.

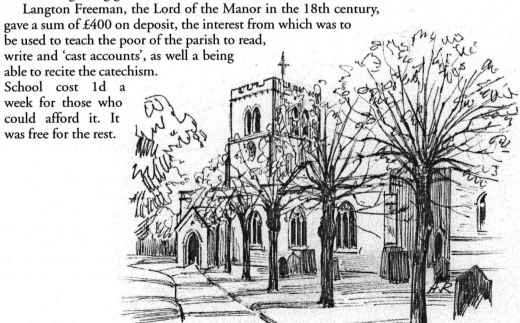

lower catesby
st mary and st edmund of canterbury

O ff the beaten track, and on the edge of this small settlement, the present church is relatively new. The Catesbys, Lower and Upper, have a long and fascinating history. About 1175 Robert Esseby, Lord of the Manor, founded a Cistercian Priory in the village of Lower Catesby. As with many such foundations, the church came under control of the prioress and her nuns. Within a relatively short time, the population had already begun to decline as the Priory acquired more and more land. The Priory survived until the Dissolution in 1536, when the buildings were pulled down, the land sold off. The Onley family built a large house with extensive gardens on almost the same site that the priory had occupied.

The church is surrounded by a ha ha, a dry ditch that stops sheep getting into the churchyard. Entrance is through an open sided wooden porch at the west end of the building. The present church was built between 1861 and 1862 as a chapel for the Attenborough family of Catesby House. The architect was Gillet of Leicester. The building has a long nave, with no aisles, and a western bell cote, which houses one bell.

The furniture in St. Mary's came from the medieval church that stood in the churchyard at Upper Catesby – other furniture came from the old church at Catesby. The sedilia and piscina are original, crafted around 1300. The piscina has crocketted gables and pinnacles. The Jacobean pulpit has a tester, and Jacobean panels with some intricate carvings can also be seen in the reader's

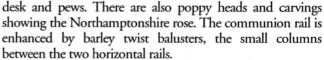

desk and pews. There are also poppy heads and carvings showing the Northamptonshire rose. The communion rail is enhanced by barley twist balusters, the small columns between the two horizontal rails.

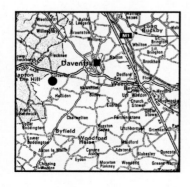

The glass in the square east windows is colourful array of saints. Some of the glass in the wset windows dates from the 14th and 15th centuries. The delightful altar cloth was hand-made by the Attenborough family. The church contain few memorials, but there is a brass to the Attenboroughs and a hatchment to the Parkhursts. A board reveals that Charles Parkhurst gave money in trust to purchase coal for the poor of the parish.

lower shuckburgh
st john the baptist

One of the striking features when driving through this small village on the A425 from Daventry to Southam is the highly elaborate church. Standing just off the main road, the small building was built in 1864 and dedicated to St. John the Baptist. Dubbed a 'Gothic temple' by one writer, it was created by Victorian church architect Croft.

Along a path leading to the door, the eye-catching tower is evident. Elaborate, almost flamboyant, it is not untypical of Victorian architecture. The tower, capped with an equally adorned spire, sits at the south-west of the church. At its base, the building has been arranged as six deep hexagons. Inside, the tower houses a ring of three bells, brought from other churches, two cast by Hugh Watts, and bearing the dates 1601 and 1628, the other (undated) the work of Thomas Newcombe.

The ceiling of the tower is unusual in that its vaulted roof is covered with tiles that carry eastern stars, and the first impression is of a Hindu temple. The rest of the church carries the flamboyancy evident on the outside. The nave, with its two narrow aisles, has large wide piers that are almost over-burdened by what looks like imitation brickwork.

The Gothic pews have not escaped the same, almost extravagant, design, containing what appear to be excessively large poppy-heads. However, if all this is over-indulgent, the chancel has not been touched in the same way. The neat, rib-vaulted cells are covered with tiles exhibiting the same apparent imitation brickwork as seen in the arches.

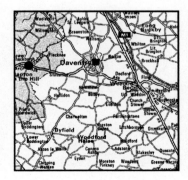

A delightful stone reredos that stands beneath it, and which has interlinking Gothic arches, enhances the east window, with its three step lancets.

It has already been said that the bells and some other features of the church have come from others places. This is also true of the font, the oldest current possession in the building. A round tub, it dates back to the 13th century, and is completed by flat arches without decoration.

maidford
st peter and st paul

The village of Maidford is sited just off what used to be a busy B-road linking Northampton with Banbury. With the opening of the M40, however, the A43 was upgraded, and this particular route de-classified, so it is now far less busy than a decade ago. The church is tucked away just off the main street. The distinctive 13th century buttressed west tower still retains its original saddleback roof. (Saddleback roofs are the same shape as an ordinary house's gabled timbers roof.) It is worth taking a look at the windows of the tower, which vary as to where they occur on the faces of the tower.

On the wall above the south door entrance to the church there is a tablet in memory of Elizabeth Goff, who died in 1883. On either side of the south entrance porch that leads into the church there are medieval carvings. The porch has a timber roof, and light enters through lancet windows with trefoils. This part of the building was restored in 1975 in memory of Henry Deterding.

Inside this compact church there is an air of peace and tranquillity. Like the tower, the south aisle is 13th century, and features a timber roof. The aisle has a three-bay arcade, and double chamfered arches enhance the octagonal piers. The top of the two lights of the screen are attached to the responds of the chancel arch. (The responds are the half piers which act as supports to hold the chancel arch.)

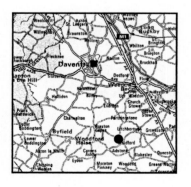

The south aisle has a clerestory fitted with plain glass, and there is a small wooden vestry at the west end of the north aisle. The arch to the tower has been blocked in with a wooden and glass screen. The chancel was re-roofed in 1954 in memory of Alice Maud Webb, who died on 9 May 1953. There is one memorial to Samson White AM, a former Rector. The memorial also includes his daughters Anne, Harriet, Emma and Maria, together with his wife Hannah. The benches, with Perpendicular style of carving, are quite plain, and were brought from nearby Eydon church.

The east window in the chancel, which has a picture of

Christ, is made from brightly colourful glass. The east window in the south wall also has vividly coloured glass, and is in memory of Arthur William Grant, who died in December 1878. It shows Jesus in the boat in rough seas, and with his frightened disciples. With the exception of these two stained glass windows, the rest of the glass in the church is either plain or engraved, and bears a variety of designs.

As in most churches, there is a memorial here to those who died in both the First and Second World Wars. The organ is housed in the former north aisle chapel, and the electric blower for the organ was put in for Arthur Boot who, in 1961, had completed 50 years as organist.

The colourful hatchment-like design bearing the words *Dieu et Mon Droit* was painted by J. C. Collins in 1813, along with the lion and unicorn with the words *honi soit qui mal y pense*. The neat, ornately carved font stands on a quadrilateral pillar, which has a hexagonal base.

newnham
church of st michael and all angels

This delightful village, with its charming thatched cottages and olde worlde charm, is an attractive place for visitors. The spire of St Michael's and All Angels church is a landmark from most directions from which the village is approached. In the past, the church was always a chapel of the parent church of Badby, and so was known as Badby-cum-Newnham. The vicar always resided in Badby, with Newnham having a curate from time to time. Prior to the Reformation, the Abbey of Evesham owned both Badby and Newnham.

Wander through the gate and you walk along a cobbled path – shaded on one side by lime trees – which is now part of the Nene Way long distance footpath, and which starts at nearby Badby and finishes at Wansford near Peterborough. The building has a unique late 14th or early 15th century buttressed bell tower, open on three sides. Supported by three arches, it is a constant reminder that at one time the bells were rung in the open at ground level from the battlemented tower. Here people, either coming to worship or walking along the street, could see the bellringers in action. The bell ropes went through holes in the roof above the heads of the bellringers. Now, after modifications, the campanologists no longer have to brave the elements. It appears, however, that the tower has not always been open, and was originally enclosed to form a ringing chamber. Baker, in his *History of Northamptonshire* (1820), shows the arches filled with masonry.

The open nature of the tower may give the impression that here there was a west porch, and indeed there is a door into this part of the church. The double chamfered wide arches of the former ringing space have been built from an attractive pink and brown stone. Above, the ceiling has a wide rib vault with ridge ribs, and a gaping bell hole. In Victorian times work was carried out to strengthen the tower, as a result of which there is a rare example of Victorian cast ironwork, in which large tie rods and anchor plates were used. There is a niche with its nodding ogee (double curve) to the west, and within the tower there are four 'Y' shaped bell openings. A recessed spire sits neatly on top of the tower, and it has two tiers of lucarnes (dormer windows).

Access to the church is through a half-circular entrance, above which is a sundial stone. Inside the 17th century porch there are two windows, but it is without the usual low seats. Turn around and admire the views above the village and across the rolling Northamptonshire landscape. From the south porch, entry to the church proper is through a 15th century Perpendicular south door, on the stonework of which are carved two rows of floral arrangements. The present nave, north aisle and chancel all date from the 1500s, and are on the site of a former 12th century chapel. The only known remains from this earlier building is a 12th century arch that can now be found in the vestry.

The four bays of arches in the nave are of Decorated style, with single chamfered octagonal piers supporting those in the south aisle. Of the piers in the north aisle, the two westerly ones have quatrefoils; the other two are octagonal. The arches in the north arcade are similar to those found in the southern section. It has been suggested that the marks on the east pillar, on the outside of the aisle, show the position of the earlier three-decker pulpit.

During the same period as the tower was constructed, additions were made to the interior of the building. A south aisle was added, the eastern section of the north aisle was rebuilt, and a pillar was added in this area. The windows also date from this period, and are in Perpendicular style. During the extensive work, the roof covering both chancel and nave was raised, and the present eight clerestory windows which were added – four on either side with gold and white glass – can be seen above the arcade of arches. These have remained unaltered since they were installed. The roof beams also date from this period.

Also at this time, the tower was capped with a medieval spire, and apart from the addition of the 17th century porch and a vestry in the 19th century, the building has remained virtually unchanged since that time.

However, as with so many churches, the 19th century 'meddlers' intervened, and made a number of alterations. These included the replacement of the middle and south-west windows in the south aisle and the middle windows in the north aisle, all of which were reproduced in a pseudo-Decorated style. Earlier glass in seven of the windows was replaced with new stained glass, including the east window of the chancel. The west window in the south aisle has a variety of stained glass, which depicts eagles, a lion, unicorn, angel and the Lamb of God. The two lights have scenes from the Bible, with the left one showing Pentecost, the right one the Crucifixion. It has been suggested that this 14th century west window may originally have been in a different part of the church. The westerly windows in both the south and north aisles are identical, although the glass designs vary. In both windows the lower lights are similar, and those in the south aisles surrounded by acorns and oak leaves. The east window in the south wall has some elegant Perpendicular tracery, and the two central stained glass figures are those of St. Peter, holding a key, and St. Michael, who bears a sword. The latter is protected by a variety of other saints. The upper light of the same window shows a host of golden angels. Some fragments of earlier yellow glass still remain in the upper lights. A variety of saints and angels can be seen in light coloured stained glass of the north aisle's east window, which also has Perpendicular tracery.

The glass in the window of the five-light east chancel window has a variety of shields and emblems. In the centre there is a plain cross, and there is a large symbolic golden key on the left, representing the one that will open the gates of heaven. It bears the inscription *Open ye the gates of Righteousness*. Also on the right is the staff of life, with the words "feed my lamb". Further symbols include an eagle, St. Michael (the church's patron saint), a communion chalice and the coat of arms of the Thornton and Newenham families. The other chancel windows contain plain glass. The top of the east window in the north aisle has been renovated, and shows the coat of arms of Thomas Newenham. who died in 1542.

> *In days gone by the box pews were leased to principal village householders. Those who could afford the most rents had the best view of proceedings. Pew rents were still in existence during the 19th century renovations, and an additional number of box pews added to bring the total to thirty-seven. However, provision was made for poorer people, and a number of free benches were installed in the nave. These have since been replaced with the present pews. Older pews include the vestry pew, situated in the north-west corner, which had separate seats for the officials.*

The usual features of the chancel are also evident in Newnham Church. There is stone sedilia and piscina, and these – together with the arches and windows – all owe their existence to early 14th century craftsmen. A priest's door can also be found here.

In 1634, John Thornton acquired the Lordship of the Manor from the Knightleys of Fawsley, and this Brockhall family became prominent in the village for several centuries. A monument in the chancel commemorates Thomas Thornton, who died in 1632, and his wife Elizabeth, who passed away in 1604. Two monuments to members of the Blacklock family –

both soldiers – are also in the chance. John is on the north wall and William on the south. Members of the Hickman family have memorials on the north wall by the north door, and on the same wall – towards the east – it is the Marriotts who are remembered.

The addition of choir stalls took place in 1894, and an organ was added in 1912. Two gravestones were brought in from the churchyard to be included in a panel when work was carried out to the reredos. The up-to-date gas heating system came in 1971, a replacement for the boilers that had provided underfloor heating in the building since the 19th century.

Although the pulpit only dates from the 18th century, above it is a 15th century brass to the memory of Lelitia Catesby, placed here for safe-keeping. She was originally married to John Newenham, but when he died she remarried Robert Catesby. He died in 1647, and a brass was put down in his memory. However, this was removed from the church during the 17th century.

When you have enjoyed the beauty of the interior of St. Michael's and All Angels, it's worth spending some time in the churchyard. Here it is possible to ponder events past. When there was no longer any space in the churchyard for burials, an extension was incorporated, which took in the playground of the former village school, next door. The present school on Church Hill superseded this, and the village hall now makes use of the former building.

From the churchyard the line of the original thatched roof can be seen on the east wall immediately below the turret. This was altered when the 15th century additions were made, to include the clerestory. It was flattened, with lead being added to make it high enough to put in the clerestory.

norton
church of all saints

The church is just off the well used unclassified road that links Daventry with the A5, and then via Whilton Locks to Northampton. Although not immediately obvious from the main road, the delightful building is worth searching out. As with many churches, a great deal of rebuilding has taken place over the centuries, though much of what remains dates from the 14th century.

The south entrance is reached along a flagged path flanked by pollarded lime trees, enabling visitors to get a good view of the west tower. It is this which contains some of the oldest parts of the building, the lower stages dating from the 13th century. At one time, this lower stage had four windows, but they have been filled in. The area above the belfry floor was added later in Perpendicular style, and is adorned with battlements.

The ring of five bells contained within the tower all date from the same year, 1640, which is quite unusual. They were cast by Hugh Watts at his bellfoundry in Leicester. The treble bell cracked and was recast in 1960, and the opportunity was taken to restore the rest of them. The roof line of the nave has been lowered and covered with copper. A line on the east side of the tower shows where the original, much steeper roof was located.

The church is entered through the 15th century porch, which leads to the south door. It is believed that the door – and that in the north wall – dates from the 16th century, with restoration taking place in 1986.

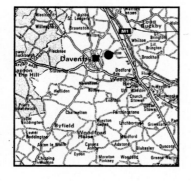

There are small capitals to the shafts on the south doorway, decorated with a variety of faces. Inside the building there is a feeling of lightness and space. The balsa model of the church on the table inside the door gives an impression of the scale of the building.

Above and round the door are six hatchments. Like most painted materials, these degenerate, so those in Norton church have been carefully restored with help of a local artist and some ladies of the village. Now showing their original colours, they are an important feature of All Saints Church. Of the hatchments on display, the oldest is to Eliab Breton, who died in 1785, and the rest – in chronological order – are for Mary Breton (1764), Michael Harvey Breton (1798), Beriah Botfield (1813), Charlotte Botfield (1825) and (a second) Beriah Botfield (1863).

The small centrally placed door opens into the tower. The Royal Arms of Queen Anne, bearing the date 1709, hang from the south wall of the tower. Once hanging in the space behind the organ (before it was installed), it was relocated to its new position so that it could be on view.

The imposing long nave features two Decorated arcades, each of which has six bays. These are held aloft on columns made up of quatrefoils. The bases of the arches are chamfered, and interesting faces peer down from these pillars at the junction of the arches. Some of the carvings are pleasant; others almost threatening and ugly. It is easy to imagine that the stonemason who carved these may have used his artistic license to portray people he knew!

High in the nave are the clerestory windows. They date from the 16th century, and were placed as high as possible to catch the sunlight. There are four on the north, and six on the south side, the sunniest side of the church. Although both north and south

All Saints has a stone-faced clock on the tower's lower stage, which is supported by a corbel. A modern, electrically driven clock has replaced the original hand-wound movement. Apart from these, there has been a variety of clocks spanning many centuries of Norton church. A scratch clock – also called a mass clock – can be seen on the jamb (upright) of the south-west window next to the south porch. In the form of a sundial, this mass clock showed the time of mass or church services. Another sundial, produced at a much later date, is on the south-west corner of the parapet, and close to the tower.

arcades are in Decorated style, the south aisle was constructed in the early part of the 14th century; the north aisle a little later in the same century. The piers that support the north arcade are octagonal; those for the south are quatrefoil. The reason for the delay in building the two aisles will never really be known, but it is almost certain that the Black Death halted progress, with work resuming once the population had recovered. Towards the east end of the south aisle, the piscina indicates that the medieval altar was sited in this area. The chapel was dedicated to St. Anne, the mother of the Virgin Mary.

The aumbry, which is in the east wall of the north aisle, was used for storing the church's patent (the plate which held the communion bread) and chalice. Now no longer used for this purpose, it holds displays of flowers. Like several churches, All Saints possesses two fonts, the oldest of which is circular and thought to be 13th century, probably reworked in the 18th century. It stands to the west side of the south door. From its surface, four protruding faces keep an eye on those present. This font has been repositioned, and is still used for baptisms. The other font, which is much smaller and fashioned from marble, is of the baluster type, the bowl being held in a scalloped base. It is thought to have come from Norton Hall.

The west screen, which consists of three storeys, is the same height as the nave. It is adorned with pilasters (bars) and arches. The upper part was formerly the reredos, and dates from the 1700s; the bottom part was produced in 1810. As in many churches, the side panels have the Lord's

Prayer, Creed and Ten Commandments, although the latter are hidden by the west gallery and 18th century organ. The oak pulpit is 17th century and Jacobean. At one time it stood much higher, being positioned at the top of several steps.

One of the highlights of St. Mary's is its stained glass. The colourful heraldic glass portrays some of the history of the church, together with the story of many of the noble families associated with its past. There is an excellent explanation of this in the church. The second Beriah Botfield presented the stained glass in the windows in both aisles to the church. These feature the four patron saints of the British Isles, and their emblems and banners are incorporated in the design. Two other saints are also shown – St. George is in the east window of the south aisle, and next to him (to the west) is St. Patrick, with St. Edmund, King of the Angles and martyr of the church, on the west side of the south door. In the north aisle, St. Andrew is towards the east, and on the left is St. David, with St. Stephen, the first Christian martyr, on the west side of the vestry.

The church also possesses a number of other attractive stained glass windows. The east window bears the signature of Willement and the date 1847; it is tall with three lancets. The three figures in this brightly coloured, some might argue gaudy, window are of our Lord with two of his disciples – St. Peter and St. Paul – on either side. It was probably installed not long after the new chancel was completed. Thomas Willement (1786–1871) was an heraldic artist to George IV, and also produced stained glass for Queen Victoria. There are also window panels at the end of the aisles, and these give an interesting chronological story of the history of the Manor.

Apart from the easily recognisable windows, there are a number of pieces of stained glass in some of the other windows, showing single figures and shields. One of the other informative features of this church are the superbly executed family trees giving the lineage of several local families, including the Bretons and Verneys.

There are two brasses in the south aisle. The first is to William and Catherine Knyght, who died in 1501 and 1504, respectively. The brass shows two 23 in (58 cm) figures. The second brass is to Ann Ward, who died in 1631, the wife of William Ward who was vicar of Norton. In the south aisle the most notable monument is to a family with historic links with the village. Although the Knightleys had their seat of power at Fawsley Hall, some six or seven miles away, they also had associations with Norton, when Sir Richard built the Hall. (This survived until blown up in an army exercise in 1945.) Lady Elizabeth Knightley was Sir Richard Knightley's second wife, and before her marriage was Elizabeth Seymour, the daughter of the Duke of Somerset, who later became Lord Protector of England. Lady Elizabeth's death occurred in 1602, a year before that of Elizabeth I. Her memorial takes the form of a large alabaster standing

Although several churches in and around Daventry are well-endowed with a variety of monuments, Norton seems to possess more than its fair share, and these add to greatly the building's interest. Although many inscriptions are brief, these memorials, spanning a period of 350 years, offer much to all those interested in the past. From these glimpses of past traditions, it is possible to piece together a great deal about the history of this fascinating village and its inhabitants.

monument, on which she is shown as a recumbent effigy wearing a distinctive pointed head-dress, her hands in prayer. The effigy is protected beneath a canopy, and the monument is elaborately decorated with large black columns on either side, together with outer obelisks. A variety of symbols adorn the tablet, including the family coat of arms and a skull, as well as two golden acorns, an axe and a hoe, with a chain which links them together. Though of great interest, Pevsner dismissed it as "Not of specially high quality".

Of the two floor slabs, one is to Lucretia Duncomb, who died in 1741, the wife of a former vicar. The second slab is to the memory of William Hebden (1819), his vicar brother John (1820) and their mother Catherine (1820). The east window of the south aisle shows the Knightley coats of arms, and is for Sir Richard Knightley who died in 1615, and Lady Elizabeth Seymour. The informative details tell us that she was "the 4th daughter of Edward Duke of Somerset, Protector of England and Uncle to King Edward ye 6th". She died in 1602, and this is the second monument to her memory, the alabaster tomb also commemorating her death.

There are three memorials on the north wall in the chancel. The square tablet marks the early death of Dudley Knightley, who died in 1602 aged 19, the same year as Elizabeth his mother. The second tablet is to Ann Breton, who died in 1635. It consists of banded pieces of tapering stone (obelisks) on both the left and right. There is an open semi-circular arch (pediment) with segments, and it also features a skull and the arms of Verney. The third memorial here, of white marble, is to Charlotte Botfield, who died in 1825, and is the work of William Behnes. She is shown leaning on her right elbow on the altar-like tomb, using her left hand to support her head. She mourns her son Beriah (the younger). One authority (K. A. Esdaile) says that the carving on this memorial is better than any produced by the well-known sculptor Flaxman, and as he notes, "...it conveys a real emotion and is nobly carved".

There are also memorials to various members of the Breton family on the south wall. The memorial to Captain Nicholas Breton, who died in 1624, shows his arms. The memorial takes the form of a tablet with two cherubs, and is in subdued style. Although it is Jacobean, some

experts suggest that it would not be considered to "fit this era". Another monument on the same wall is to a second Nicholas Breton, who died in 1658, and his memory lives on in the form of a large standing monument. His wife, Elizabeth Knight, is also commemorated with a large monument, and like the monument to Captain Breton, some believe it owes its design to a later age. In the centre there are two busts, and a large surround of white and pink marble. The open pediment is made up of a number of segments, and has a shield and garlands. Above this, the arms of the Breton family impale those of the Knight family. The Latin inscription, when translated, means "He left a reputation which will long endure among future generations."

The north aisle also has a number of monuments. At the east end is a monument showing a large kneeling figure, and enhanced with broad piers and three allegorical figures. This is to Elizabeth Verney, who died in 1633, and takes the form of an open pediment. The arms of Verney are shown, and on a square black tablet there are a further 20 painted shields, indicating the relationships between the Verneys and other families – including the Cheyney, Darcy, Willoughby, de Broke, Beauchamp and Greville families. Restoration work was carried out to the monument in 1975.

A white and grey marble tablet recalls the death of Beriah Botfield in 1813. We are told that "He embellished the adjacent mansion" and "ameliorated [improved] the moral condition of the neighbouring poor". There is a memorial to a second Beriah Botfield (the younger), who died in 1863, MP for Ludlow. We can read on his epitaph, "The treasures of human intellect may outlive the memory of him who gathered them together at Norton". Further tablets in the same aisle are to Richard Bliss, who died in 1864, and James Lovelock, who died in 1952.

Outside the church, the Botfields have been buried in the south-east corner of the churchyard. When there was not enough space, the Botfields made arrangements to have the area enlarged, which they did on two occasions. Railings surround their burial space, and their tomb chests are engraved with their coats of arms.

preston capes
church of st peter and at paul

The village of Preston Capes has resisted modern innovations, and it still does not have street lighting, which is partly why it retains a degree of original rural charm. The church, off the main street, sits on the edge of the village, with the Northamptonshire countryside coming up to its boundary. From its tower there are views across the undulating landscape, including Fawsley with it former Knightley family seat. As with several other villages in the area, there are historical links at Preston Capes with this once influential local family here in the village and church.

Each church has its own peculiarities. With Fawsley it is its location in a field; for Braunston the almost awe-inspiring spire. The initial impression when approaching the Church of St. Peter and St. Paul at Preston Capes is that the various parts of the church appear to be out of proportion. Some remnants of Perpendicular tracery can be seen on the bell opening, which are made up two-lights, and which have transoms (cross-beams). The appearance of the tower is made more attractive by its crowing, well-proportioned battlements. Five bells hang in the tower, producing an attractive peal, two of which are dated 1631, and one of which weighs just over 8 cwt (around 900 lbs); the other over 6 cwt (670 lbs).

When Bridges was collecting information for his *History of Northamptonshire*, he recorded that a Mr W. Taylor made some remarks about the bells of Preston Capes (and East Haddon), and indicated that he had "Accounted two famous rings of bells as tuneable and musical as any within five miles of them".

As with many churches constant ringing – together with ravages of age and disease – weakened the wooden frames in which the Preston Capes bells hung. In 1922 a new steel frame was provided, and the cost of rehanging these heavyweights was borne by the Rector as a thank you for the great effort which local people had made to raise money for re-roofing the nave in 1921.

The church is entered through the south door, with

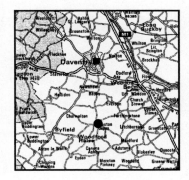

its unusually shaped stone archway, in which there is a memorial to the fallen of the 1914–18 war. The out of proportion impression of the building is partly because various parts were added at different times. In the case of St. Peter and St. Paul, the relatively large west tower was built into the westerly bay of the nave, taking up space. This tends to give the impression that the church is quite small, borne out once inside the building. However, this does not detract from the attractive, well-cared for place of worship. By looking at the west end of the nave, and especially the half arches, it is possible to see how the building of the tower impinged upon the earlier nave. Up above in the nave there are four plain almost square clerestory windows on each side.

Of the two aisles in the church, the arcade in the south one dates from the mid-12th century. The arcade is of two and a half bays, and the large circular pillars have arches which are slightly pointed. The north arcade is thought to have been constructed some two centuries later, and its two and a half arcade bays show double chamfered arches, resting on well-proportioned stylish octagonal piers. There is a distinct contrast in the colours and nature of the material used for the north and south aisles. Light-coloured limestone was used for the north arcade, with dark ironstone used in the south arcade. Where the arches join the columns, the work of earlier craftsmen has produced some intriguing and ornately carved corbels. Careful examination shows that each of these is different – they are each said to represent one of the eight King Henrys.

As with so many churches, restoration work has been carried out at various times. In 1853 work took place on the chancel, at which time it was raised by almost two feet, making it that much higher than the nave roof. This work also allowed the then almost flat roof to be raised by about the same amount. On the inside of the arched roof supports there are a number of richly decorated floral panels.

Unlike many fonts that are free-standing, the Perpendicular one in the Church of St. Peter and St. Paul has been built into the

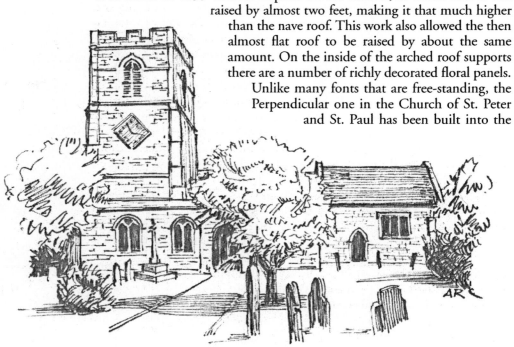

nave's westerly pillar. The font has a range of tracery panels, which are reminiscent of those usually found in windows. The small, now disused, piscina is to be found on the north side of the chancel's arch. Earlier pews in the church were removed and replaced by the present ones when other restoration work was carried out in 1853. At the same time, the pulpit and prayer desk, both in Gothic style, were also introduced. There is an inscription on the pulpit, which reads "Go ye into all the world and preach the gospel to every creature".

All the windows in the church are either coloured or filled with stained glass, and even those with no long history to tell have multi-coloured panes that add an extra dimension to the already attractive building. The windows with pieces of multi-coloured, diamond shaped pieces of glass are referred to as 'harlequin' windows. In addition to the plain windows, those with stained glass have pictures or tell stories. The circular panel of the tower's west window is a good example, featuring a colourful interpretation of The Last Supper. The small window which graces the chancel's north wall is probably 12th century in origin, and the delightful patterns which are created on the wall opposite when the sun shines are produced by the very bright red and blue stained glass.

Other windows are more modern and were installed for specific purposes. The east window shows very little of the tracery which was completed during Victorian times. In fact, this stained glass window was neglected, and as with the others it was in need of repair. The present window, with its superbly executed designs by Annabel Rathbone, was put in place in 1974. These are engraved onto plain glass. The window was erected to the memory of 10 year old George St. John Ravenshear, who died in 1972, and whose headstone is on the east side of the churchyard. Family and friends paid for the engraved window, which depicts a variety of stories. Part of it shows St. Peter and St. Paul, to whom the church is dedicated. The same window also includes an early symbol of Christ, known as the 'chicriho' (P) and the centre light reveals a peacock. The bird was placed over human tombs in the catacombs and signified everlasting life. The Eucharist, confirming that flesh is incorruptible, forms part of the design. In addition, there are three trees – olive, cypress and cedar – which, although found as imports in Britain, have Biblical significance. Various birds, including doves, owls and peacocks, can be seen perched in the trees, and underneath sheep, rabbits, lambs, a hedgehog and a beetle, together with a deer – the latter a symbol of meditation – have been included. The left panel has a picture of the heavenly city of Jerusalem, which also includes St. George and the dragon, the face of St. George being that of George Ravenshear. Above all this at the top of the window, heavenly angels hover around the seraphim in coloured glass.

Still in the sanctuary, the painted boards placed behind the altar include the Creed, The Lord's Prayer and the Ten Commandments. The coat of arms, typical of many churches, can still be found. It features the fleur-de-lis (a reminder of the English claim to France), a lion, and the ubiquitous unicorn which supports the coat of arms.

The church does not contain any monuments, though there are a number of memorial tablets. One of these, on the south wall of the chancel, commemorates the Rev. Knightley Adam, an 18th century vicar. His wife, Jane, was the only child of Dr Richard Newton, who was responsible for founding Hertford College, Oxford. The plaque also remembers three of his four sons, who all died relatively young died between 1741 and 1753 – Samuel was nine months, Robert eight years and Richard 26 years old. Opposite is a small lance-shaped window containing vivid purple and red glass that floods the church with colour when the sun shines.

The village of Preston Capes has resisted modern innovations, and it still does not have street lighting, which is partly why it retains a degree of original rural charm. The church, off the main street, sits on the edge of the village, with the Northamptonshire countryside coming up to its boundary. From its tower there are views across the undulating landscape, including Fawsley with it former Knightley family seat. As with several other villages in the area, there are historical links at Preston Capes with this once influential local family here in the village and church.

The Knightleys, as in several other local villages, were benefactors to the poor, and were responsible for setting up the village school, as well as being patrons of the living. A brass on the wall opposite commemorates the Rev. Valentine Knightley, who at the age of 86 had served the parish of Preston Capes as Rector for some 62 years. In addition, the Rector's parishioners and friends also provided an organ in his memory.

There are memorial tablets to Mrs Elizabeth Meek, daughter of the Rev. Mr Richard Knightley, Rector of Byfield and Charwelton, and dated 1737. Another is to the memory of Edward Sorrill, who died in 1722. Several slabs sunk into the nave floor commemorate the past lives of various members of the Butler family.

The earlier craft of the woodcarver is shown in the choir stall, where characteristic poppy heads can be seen. On the walls around the bell tower there are a number of boards that record various notable occasions when the bells have been rung.

Apart from a number of interesting graves in the churchyard, some of which date back to the 1600s, the base of a former preaching cross remains to the south east side of the church's porch. It was around this cross that people gathered to worship before the church building was erected. The head of the cross has been included in the east wall of the chapel.

staverton
church of the blessed virgin mary

Staverton, now protected by a bypass, is no longer subject to the continuous onslaught of the busy A425 that wound its way through the narrow roads of this delightful village. Peace has returned to this picturesque settlement, with its ironstone buildings, standing but a few miles from the Warwickshire border.

The main body of the church dates from the early 14th century, the only older part being the north doorway that exhibits a round arch in a simple design. Once inside, and especially standing within the nave, there is an immediate air of spaciousness. Dating from about 1300, it has an arcade of seven low and narrow bays, its arches displaying hollow chamfers, held on octagonal piers. Other features which also date from the 1300s include the finely crafted east window in the north aisle and one of the south windows.

The most noticeable feature of the church is the extremely large and substantial Perpendicular tower, crowned by distinctive battlements. It has pairs of imposing two-light transomed bell openings, and contains an excellent ring of six bells, the oldest from 1662. The 1676 bell owed its original manufacture to Baglee of Chacombe. Three of the other bells are 18th century – 1720, 1726 and 1776. Both the fourth and tenor bells bore inscriptions and the date 1662. The bells were hung in a new frame in 1839. In 1938 the five bells were removed from the tower and taken to the bellfoundry of John Taylor & Co, Loughborough, where they were melted down, and from the five bells, six recast. It would appear at one time that Staverton had a bell cast at the foundry of Richard Keene which included the date 1662.

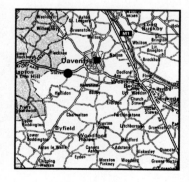

The North chapel is in Decorated style, and its three bays, like those of the north aisle, feature octagonal piers, although the arches have double-hollow chamfered arches. The panel tracery in one of the south aisle windows entirely fills the top half, and similar tracery of reticulated style can be found in the east window of the chancel. Because it is drawn in circles, and extended to produce s-shape curves, it gives a net-like appearance.

In the south wall, which divides the Lady Chapel from the chancel, there is a both a sedilia and piscina with large ogee arches. Closer scrutiny of the seat of the sedilia reveals a number of marks which, according to tradition, were made by the swords of the army passing by either before or after the Battle of Naseby. The dominating feature of the south wall is the tall Perpendicular window, filled with stained glass bearing the images of a number of people, including Christ, St. Peter and St. Paul, above whom there are smaller figures representing the twelve apostles. Close by there is a smaller, 13th century window, the glass showing fishermen working their nets in the sea of Galilee. The cross keys of St. Peter are also included.

In the church's north wall, the most westerly window has stained glass figures representative of faith, hope and charity. The stained glass in the east window is of a much later date, installed in 1903. Inscribed with the words "Behold the hand maid of the Lord", it portrays scenes of Mary and the Crucifixion. The glass in the chancel's south window has emblems that make up the coat of arms of Christchurch College in Oxford, and these share the window with the John Bull and Cardinal Wolsey's hat.

The church also contains a number of memorials, including one to "The memory of Rev Everard Slade Powell, MA, scholar of Christchurch College in Oxford and Vicar of Staverton from 1933–46 and Ringing Master of the Peterborough Diocesan Guild of Church Bellringers from 1935 to 1947. Requiescat in peace". It was the Rev. Powell who was responsible for the re-casting and rehanging of the bells.

Another Rector of Staverton, William Chase, who provided pastoral oversight for the people of the village for some 30 years, has a memorial to his memory, which records that he died in 1935 at the age of 72.

Close to the east window in the north chapel, known as the Lady Chapel, there is a large statue of the Virgin Mary. This particular part of St. Mary's Church was originally dedicated to St. Catharine of Alexandra, and a statue of the saint filled the position which the Blessed Virgin now occupies. On the ledge on the side of the same window there used to be a Catharine wheel.

The oldest monument is on the north wall of the Chapel, and is to the memory of Thomas Wylmer, who died in 1580. A large standing monument, it has two short ionic columns with – to quote the correct architectural terms – a metope frieze with wide metopes. A brass plate in the middle of the monument is engraved with kneeling figures.

stowe nine churches

st michael and all angels church stowe

Like so many churches, the building has been erected in an excellent position on the brow of a hill in Church Stowe, which before 1717 was known as Great Stow. The church was dedicated to St. Michael in 1560, having previously been dedicated to St. Ninian and then to St. Peter and St. Paul. The ancient west tower, Saxon in origin, gives this church a history that goes back for more than a thousand years. Apart from the historic tower, the building also consists of a nave, north and south aisles, a chapel, south porch and chancel.

Speculation arises as to the origins of the church. According to the 11th century account of St. Werburga, written by Goscelin, Alnoth was a cowherd and serf in the Werburga's monastery in nearby Weedon. After Werburga's death Alnoth fled the village. From this time he lived the rest of his life as a hermit in the woods around Stowe, until he was set upon and killed by robbers not long after Werburga's death. He was later elevated to the sainthood. Historians believe that the original building was erected as a shrine or oratory to St. Alnoth, and possibly also to St. Werburga, coming into existence in the 8th century in a part of this settlement which had long been considered "a hallowed place".

The church is reached through an attractive lychgate erected in memory of the Rev. Charles Crawley, who held the living at Stowe for some sixty years.

The slightly leaning tower has a parapet, enhanced by pinnacles on each corner. The Saxon origins of the church are confirmed because of the lesenes (rectangular columns) which can be seen on the bell stage, close to the west and east bell openings. Further evidence for the church's Saxon origins is provided by the characteristic clasped tower arrangement of the south aisle. This embraces the tower at the east end, and is found in other Saxon churches, including those at Brigstock and Kings Sutton. When subsequent building work was being carried out, it was considered that the Saxon work was too important to obliterate, so the new sections of the

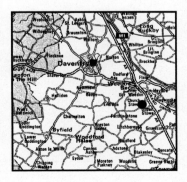

church were built around them. During excavations in 1899, Sir Henry Dryden discovered some Saxon foundations near the present pulpit.

The tower contains a peel of four bells, all of which bear inscriptions, but only three are dated. The earliest of these bells goes back to 1590, and has the inscription 'God Save our Queen'. The other two bells with dates are inscribed as 1607, and the final bell informs us that "Thomas Russell of Wootton near Bedford 1725" was responsible for it. It is worth taking a look on the outside at the parapet that runs the full length of the nave and chancel.

Entrance to the church is at present through the heavy south door, and there are some attractive decorative features on the door pillars. Leaf carvings can also be seen on the inside of the porch.

The church has a number of other interesting historical features that include the original Saxon arch separating the tower from the nave. In addition, the church has no less than seven very early carved stones, a feature that cannot be matched by any other church in Northamptonshire. Three of these stones have been incorporated into the fabric of the Anglo-Saxon west tower; the rest can be found in the Baptistry.

During renovations to the church in 1639, all the windows were removed and new square-headed windows, with their plain mullions, installed. Later restoration work in 1859 was carried out by Philip Hardwick, and included a number of features that can be found in the Lady Chapel. These include a raised roof, choir stalls, Bath-stone pillars, the font and altar. At the time this work was being carried out, certain items were removed from the church, including the medieval font, the three-decker pulpit, box pews and west-end gallery. These have never been returned to the church. However, other items which were removed at the same time – the Jacobean reredos, the 18th century altar table and the Lady Chapel screen – were brought back into the church in 1973. The reredos is now the dividing feature between the nave and chapel. There was also extensive restoration work in 1925 to the tower, carried out by the Society for the Protection of Ancient Buildings.

There are many treasures in this small village church. One of these is the ancient tomb – made of Purbeck marble – to Gerald de Lisle. He is thought to have been a Crusader Knight. On his tomb he is shown cross-legged and in a costume of chain mail, covered by a long flowing robe.

However, of all the monuments in the Church of St. Michael, undoubtedly the most attractive is that in memory of Lady Elizabeth Carey, who died in 1630. She was the mother of the Earl of Danby, and co-heiress of John Lord Latimer. The Earl of Danby received his title from Charles I in 1625, and he carried out much restoration work on the church. His mother's monument is on the south side of the altar, dividing the chancel from the south chapel. It was masterfully executed in 1620 – ten years before she died – by Nicholas Stone, the King's Master Mason. The cost was £220! Many historians – and others – are of the opinion that this particular piece of work is the best carved memorial dating from this period. Her family consisted of three sons and six daughters by her first husband Sir John Danvers.

The arms of de Lisle can be seen on a shield on the front of the tomb. It is known that in 1310 when Edward II was on the throne, Warrien de Lisle, the father of Sir Gerald, was Lord of Stowe. In 1321, Warrien unwisely took up arms against Edward. As a result he was captured at the Battle of Borough Bridge in Yorkshire, and then taken to Pontefract, where his execution took place shortly afterwards. As a result of this, the Manor of Stowe became the King's property. When son Gerald repented for his father misdemeanour by showing his loyalty to Edward, he was given back the estate. In 1327 he went with the King to wars in Scotland and in France. His death occurred in 1360.

One of the most notable people who lived in Stowe was Dr Thomas Turner, who was President of Corpus Christi College in Oxford. He erected the fellows' building in 1712. He died in 1714, and his memorial is in St. Michael's. It was commissioned by the Sons of the Clergy Corporation to mark an £18,000 legacy that Turner gave to them to buy the Manor of Stowe. The monument in the north aisle is to John Daye, Comptroller of the Foreign Post Office, and Mrs Mary Daye. His vault is under the chancel.

The south aisle's Lady Chapel has a memorial to the Rev. Charles and Mrs Mary Crawley. The Rev. Charles, Rector of Stowe from 1789 to 1849, was involved with promoting a revival of the Catholic Outlook, a forerunner to the Oxford Movement. This movement was in favour of, supported and promoted a revival of the Catholic outlook of the High Church Party in the Church of England. From the time that Charles Crawley was appointed Rector in 1789, successive members of the Crawley family held the position for the next 132 years, until 1921.

The living has a long line of incumbents, the first being Walter Sacerdot of Stowe, although the date when he took up the position of priest is not known. Hugh de Pateshall succeeded him in 1230. At one time there was a stairway that led to the gallery, but the eight-sided Victorian font now stands in the position it once occupied.

stowe nine churches
church of st james upper stowe

The small church of St. James in Upper Stowe stands behind a triangle of green, opposite to the Old Dairy Farm Centre. It is reached along a short, tree-lined concrete pathway, and backs onto fields in an open, slightly elevated position. It is much younger, and certainly relatively simpler in construction, than its Church Stowe neighbour.

Victorian in construction, it was styled by the architect P. C. Hardwick, who was also responsible for some 19th century alterations at Church Stowe. At the west end of the building a bell cote replaces the more traditional tower, and contains a small bell cast in 1855. Access to the building is through the large north timber porch, and in spite of its almost immodest nature, the church has a distinctive atmosphere. The abiding impression is of an abundance of attractive glass for such a small building. The entrance from the porch leads directly into a nave without aisles, a small chancel and a vestry off this. The bench pews are also of modest design. Because of the steepness of the roof, the nave has low walls. Exhibiting wide chancel arches, these extend virtually across the whole width of the nave.

The ornate reredos, with its delightful gold, green and red colouring, is worth a good look, as are designs on the walls of the chancel, being enhanced with quotations. All the windows take the form of lancets; that in the chancel's south wall has steeply shaped lancets, and the large east window has three bell lancets. The Victorian pulpit has some interesting carved stone panels, reminiscent of the window tracery found in many older churches. The only vestige of an earlier age appears to be the piscina in the vestry, which could be medieval.

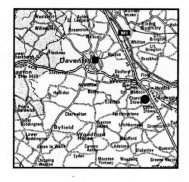

Though the church is relatively new, there is some excellent stained glass. In the east window, the figures of the apostles keep company with Jesus. Two other saints, Maria and Joseph, are shown in the stained glass in the south windows of the small sanctuary. The window opposite the vestry depicts Mary and Joseph.

upper shuckburgh
church of st john the baptist in the wilderness

The village takes its name from the Shuckburgh family, which have had their home here for centuries. The church is on the site of a former village, and is considered by some to be 'quaint'. It is situated in the well-kept grounds of Shuckburgh Hall, which can be glimpsed from the church, and is shaded and protected by an enormous Cedar of Lebanon. Unlike the church at Lower Shuckburgh, which owes its existence to creative Victorians, the estate church of St. John the Baptist has been a feature of the area for many centuries. The earliest parts are from the 13th century; the latest from the 19th.

Although the present building was erected in 1844, it stands on the site of an earlier structure. The oldest part of the church is probably the west tower, which dates back to the 13th century. A Victorian Gothic bell stage, which is topped by four pinnacles, has been added. The tower has a ring of four bells, with bells three and four bearing the inscriptions "Henry Bagley made mee 1640' and "Henry Bagley made mee 1651". The treble was a gift from Sir Richard Shuckburgh in 1657, and was recast in 1864.

Inside the church there is a nave and chancel with two chapels, both of which have elaborate roofs. The pulpit, a very ornate affair, has barley twist carvings, and also features both fruits and leaves. The lectern, brought into the church during Victorian restoration, is Gothic. There is some late 16th century heraldic stained glass in the south-west window. However, not surprisingly, it is the monuments and brasses to the Shuckburgh family that almost overwhelm this church.

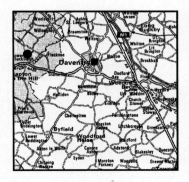

The oldest of the brasses is in the north chapel, where only part of a brass remains to Margaret Cotes (1500), and one to Thomas Shuckburgh and his wife Margaret, dated 1549. A further brass is to the memory of Sir Stukeley Shuckburgh (1759), together with a variegated marble ornament with an oval medallion.

Further brasses can be found on the south side of the chancel, including one to the memory of Anthony

Shuckburgh and his wife dated 1594. In the same part of the church is a bust to Catherine Shuckburgh, mounted on a large tablet. The monument to John Shuckburgh of 1724 is by Hunt of Northampton. It has pilasters, and at its head there are two small putti – in this case small boys – with tears in their eyes.

To the north side of the nave a monument to the memory of Lady Shuckburgh, who died in 1738, has an angel lying on an urn, which stands in front of an obelisk. Other monuments here include an 1804 mock white globe to Sir George Shuckburgh-Evelyn. Nearby, Sir Stenkley Shuckburgh has an oval relief memorial that commemorates his death in 1809. In the south chapel, the moment to John Shuckburgh and his wife bears the date 1631. There are two recumbent effigies on this stone memorial, and it includes two columns and a flat back arch with an adornment of strapwork. A circular recess holds the bust of Richard Shuckburgh, which bears the date 1656. The recess also features cherubs and trumpets. The pediment at the top has garlands and a skull. The sculptor has also included his signature.

Other memorials, mainly in the form of simple tablets, can be found in different parts of the church.

> *The church is on the site of a former village, and is considered by some to be 'quaint'. It is situated in the well-kept grounds of Shuckburgh Hall, which can be glimpsed from the church, and is shaded and protected by an enormous Cedar of Lebanon.*

watford
church of st peter and st paul

Standing in a leafy lane, and still overshadowed by the large estate wall of what was once the Jacobean mansion of Watford Court, the church of St. Peter and St. Paul is almost hidden from view – and certainly from the cars which rush along the busy B4036. It is the stately horse chestnut and yew trees in the churchyard that afford some protection to the church and that give it a special feeling of peace and tranquillity, seeming to insulate it from the intrusions of the 20th century.

Built in about 1300, the large west tower is in the Perpendicular style of architecture. It is perhaps not surprising that a tower of these proportions should have a large, eye-catching west window, with its four-lights. Heads are carved on either side, that to the south still being discernible; the one to the north less so. There are also four conspicuous bell openings, and the tower is completed with gargoyles and distinctive battlements.

The ring of six bells produces a unique tune. Five of the six bear the date 1695, and one, which was recast in 1712, was originally the work of Henry Bagley. The tenor originally bore a Latin inscription which, when translated, means "I being rung am called Mary" – it was recast in 1820.

An ancient holly keeps the gravestones company on the north side of the church, together with a number of table tombs. Ancient headstones also rest against the wall of the adjacent land. The north porch and doorway are no longer used. On the walk along the path to the ancient south porch there is a warning notice about falling masonry from the tower! There is also a sundial above this entrance. The iron gates allow access to an ancient south porch, although it has undoubtedly been rebuilt. The single lancet windows have metal supports. Figures of ancient kings keep guard over the interior of the south door.

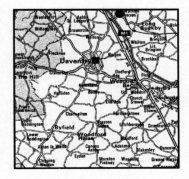

The tall, slender arch between the tower and nave is imposing, and is from the Perpendicular period. In the north aisle, another arch leads into the tower, though this is neither as lofty nor as grand as that between the nave and tower. The nave has two almost identical aisles, and their arcades each have three bays of arches. The south arcade arches, with their double chamfers, have octagonal pier capitals, and date from the Decorated period. In the north aisle, the arcades are similar to those in the south aisle – corbel heads are found at the base of both sets, and bear more than a passing likeness to a number of English kings. The high nave clerestory windows are square-headed with two lights, and contain clear glass.

The box pews in the west end of the south aisle face towards the centre of the church; those in the rest of the building towards the sanctuary. A Decorated piscina can be found in the south aisle, suggesting that there was once an altar here. The church has two fonts, both of which stand at the east end of the south aisle. One is from Victorian times, and the second of greater antiquity, stands close by. The memorial on the west wall of the south aisle is a Roll of Honour to those who fell in the 1914–18 war.

Two of the windows in the south wall of the nave have three-stepped lancet lights with plain glass. There are two identical windows on the north side of the nave. The third one has a pair of lancets, and all have intersected tracery. The north wall windows are elaborate, and in some of them both intersected and cusped tracery is visible. There is an interesting stone just to the right of the easterly window, which has a trefoil design. Close to the Victorian Gothic pulpit are some late 18th century choir pews. However, in addition to these there are some quite plain, unattractive box pews in the isles that date from the early part of the 19th century.

The small doorway close to the north wall leads into a rather large north chapel. Pause to enjoy the extremely eye-catching east window. Although it does not contain stained glass, it is the superbly executed tracery which is the appealing feature. The window has five lights each of which has two groups of Y-shaped tracery on both the left- and right-hand sides of each light. Above this is a large circle resplendent with its cinquefoil design. The ledges on either side of the window are now empty, but at one time would undoubtedly have held statues of saints. In addition to the piscina in the south aisle, another more elegant one can be seen here.

A dividing wall separates the chapel from the nave, and on the north wall there are three 14th century tomb recesses. A cursory glance at the north wall shows that two of the low arches have been blocked in, but it would appear that at one time they would have provided a link between the north chapel and the chancel. The opened-out wall safe in the north wall was possibly used as an aumbry, a small cupboard for keeping sacred vessels for mass. There is also a piscina. The oak chest is of medieval origin.

If the north chapel was attractive, it is eclipsed by the sheer size of the chancel. Here the arches inside the chapel are repeated, emphasising the link between that part of the building and the present chancel. Of almost the same length as the nave, it is also of about the same height. It is undoubtedly the most distinguishing feature of the Church of St. Peter and St. Paul. The tall chancel arch is of the Perpendicular period, and above is an oak roof of great antiquity. Even so, it is the enormous windows, together with memorials to members of the Clerk family, which give this part of the church a distinctiveness unsurpassed in the rest of the building.

The 14th century Perpendicular east window is a particularly fine example from this period, and an imposing reminder of the techniques perfected by our ancestral craftsmen. Made up of five tall lights, there is a smaller decoration at the top. The stained glass reveals an image of Christ in the centre, to the left of whom stands the Blessed Virgin Mary. The inscription reads "Mary had chosen that good part which shall not to be taken away from her". The window also shows some Biblical scenes, together with the saintly figures of Matthew, Mark, Luke and John. The golden glass that fills the window on the south side came from an idea put forward by one of the Lady Henleys. She wanted golden sunlight to be cast onto the east window, and so the glass was installed with this in mind.

Beneath the window, the piscina and triple sedilia reflect the activities of an earlier age. The communion rail, of slender proportions, is of 18th century construction. A priest's door is located in the south wall of the chancel.

The Clerks are remembered in the sanctuary, and both this family and the Henleys in the chancel. There are also memorials to the Clerk family, the Henleys and the Abbys in the chancel. The memorial to Sir George Clerke, who died in 1649, is a fine architectural treasure, without unnecessary embellishments, and consists of two black columns that support an open segmented pediment. There is a second memorial to another George Clerke, who it is thought died in 1689. He is remembered by a monument to the left of Sir George's which takes the form of Corinthian columns surmounted by an elongated urn. There is an excellent portrayal of the Henley arms on the 1935 memorial to Anthony Morton Henley.

The other stained glass windows in the chancel are also attractive. The westerly one is to Harriet, the widow of Robert, 2nd Lord Henley. The scene depicted is that of the Lord having descended from heaven, bringing with him an earthquake. The other images in the window show people cowering from the disaster. The poppyhead pews here are also worth more than a second glance.

weedon
church of st peter

Whereas many of Northamptonshire churches are easily seen from a distance, St. Peter's in Weedon is not in a prominent position on a rise, but is surrounded by the leisurely waters of the nearby Grand Union Canal on the eastern side, and by the continuously noisy main north-south railway line on the other. It has not always been like this, however, and before the arrival of these 'modern' forms of transport, the church would have had a more open aspect. Today, caught in the late evening sunlight, the delightful mellow Northamptonshire ironstone tower sets it in gentle relief against either the railway line or the canal embankment.

Perhaps not surprisingly, much of the detailed earlier history of the churches that undoubtedly preceded St. Peter's has been lost. There is a suggestion that the settlement had a wooden church in the mid-7th century, and although feasible, it is impossible to verify. If there was one, it has been suggested that it would probably have been set alight by the Danish invaders who passed that way in the 9th century. If such a church existed, another timber building would have risen from the ashes, and a record in the *Domesday Book* (1086) indicates that Weedon did in fact have a priest. There were further developments, and in the 11th century the Abbots of L'Abbaye du Notre Dame, Le Bec-Hellouin in France built a Norman church. Today, the tower is the only remnant of that earlier building.

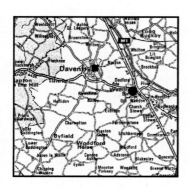

It has also been suggested that in the dim and distant past a chapel stood to the south of the site of the present church. Today there is no trace of such a building, that was dedicated to, and built after the death of, the legendary St. Werburga, who died about 700AD and – it is said – to whom the people of Weedon will always owe a debt. However, in Bridges' 18th century survey, he points out that there were still some remains of this earlier structure. According to local stories, in the past people referred to this part of the village as 'Ashyards' due, we are told, to the numerous large pieces of stone which were found in the area, and which according to tradition came from St. Werburga's chapel or abbey.

Although originally a Saxon foundation, there is nothing left from this period, and the present church, dedicated to St. Peter, owes its origins to our Norman ancestors – although the only Norman part that remains is the west tower, the walls of which are now held in place by tie-bars. The battlements on the tower add to the church's attractive appearance, but these were added in the 14th century. The large west window is also from the same period, and is Perpendicular in style.

The tower has four shafted bell openings, and there is a ring of eight bells in the tower. Although two do not bear a date, these and the others have probably been added to and undoubtedly hung and rehung during succeeding centuries. The two oldest bear the dates 1601 and 1665. In chronological order, the others are 1745, 1882, 1950 and 1951. Two other bells are not marked with dates, though the treble is dedicated as a "Memorial to those who died and who served in World War 2". Bell three has the inscription "Memorial to those who died and served in World War I", and number seven "O Son of God have mercy on me". An earlier bell with the date 1839 was recast in 1950.

> There is a suggestion that the settlement had a wooden church in the mid-7th century, and although feasible, it is impossible to verify. If there was one, it has been suggested that it would probably have been set alight by the Danish invaders who passed that way in the 9th century. If such a church existed, another timber building would have risen from the ashes, and a record in the Domesday Book (1086) indicates that Weedon did in fact have a priest.

Having passed beneath either the canal or railway bridge, the church is then reached through the main iron gate that protects the churchyard. The main path, flanked on the right with elm trees, leads to the south door. There is also one especially large yew which, if its size is anything to go by, has probably been on the site for anything up to a thousand years, and has witnessed the progression of the Christian faith over that time. Access is also possible along a path that leads from the steps down from the Grand Union Canal.

Inside the building, the low pointed and much altered tower archway is without mouldings. At one time this arch was virtually hidden by a gallery, which has since been removed. Entering through the south porch, there is an immediate feeling of space, peace and calm, in spite of the frequent trains along the nearby elevated track. This lightness of the church's interior is due in no small measure to the amount of glass in the windows, many of which contain stamped quarry glass that is the work of James Powell and Sons of Whitefriars, London. The glass in the west wall of the north and south aisles is especially delightful, with its diamond-shaped windows in an attractive mixture of green, pink and blue arranged in harlequin patterns.

In the north-west corner of the church there are some good examples of Georgian glass, and similarly dated glass can be seen above the Chapter House door. Within the south aisle, various memorial to former incumbents are positioned, together with a number of military memorials and the war memorial to the fallen. The 1860s window shows Jesus with the children, a theme found in many churches. The nave, rebuilt in 1825, is in late Georgian style, and has large round topped windows – with a wide central aisle having two arcades, each of five bays – and these have timber piers. There is an ornamental circular ventilator in the roof.

The rather small chancel came less than forty years later, when it was rebuilt in 1863 by E. F. Law, the well-known church architect, and is of the same style as the nave. The interior contains thin timber piers, with shallow narrow arched-shaped braces that connect them both longitudinally and also with the aisle walls. The window above the altar shows St. Peter, the church's patron saint, and is dedicated to the memory of a former vicar, the Rev. Idwal Lewis. The vicar's vestry, dating from 1885, completed the renovation work that began in 1823.

In the south aisle the most westerly window depicts St. Werburga. Crafted by local artist Anthony Macrae, it was dedicated on 2 May 1982 by the Bishop of Peterborough, having been erected to the Goff family in commemoration of a hundred years of service to the church by various members of the family.

St. Werburga, who lived in a monastery in the village, will always be immortalised by the legend of the geese. The people of the village were so pestered with geese that whatever they planted, the geese devoured it. Desperate to get rid of the birds, the villagers appealed to Werburga to do something. She sent out one of her serfs to round up the birds, told them of the villagers' concern, and asked them to leave and never return. As a punishment for their crimes, the geese were shut up for the night. When they were released the next day, it was found that one of the birds had vanished. Eventually it was recovered from a servant who had fancied it as a tasty meal. Satisfied that their numbers were now complete, the geese left peacefully and – according to legend

– they have never stepped foot on one of Weedon's fields since. To perpetuate the legend, the weather vane on the church tower has also been fashioned in the shape of a goose!

There are a number of other stained glass windows in the church. The one in the north aisle – the middle window from the north door – is dedicated to the Rev. John Saumarez-Winter. The east window from 1864 depicts the Good Shepherd.

The organ has been in the church since 1961, and it was bought with money raised by the local congregation and also by men from the garrison stationed in the village. It stands as a memorial to the Military Equitation Schools at Weedon Bec and Saugor in India.

The miniature small black font, which has found a home in the north aisle near the east window, was brought from the Weedon Army Ordnance Chapel in the village, and was modelled on a similar font in Winchester Cathedral. This part of the church also contains a number of military memorials.

An interesting feature of the church is the children's altar that stands in the Children's Chapel. This has been in position in the church since 1947, when pews were removed to accommodate it. The dedication was carried out by the Rev. C. Aylen, who was Vicar of Flore, and who was later made a Bishop.

The latest addition to St. Peter's Church was made in 1969, when the Chapter House was added to the north side of the church. Built from beautiful Cotswold stone, it takes the traditional octagonal chapter house shape. In summer it is possible to pause a while to have refreshments served from here. The Chapter House is reached from inside the church through the north door. Dedicated by the Rt. Reverend Bill Westwood, Bishop of Peterborough, it contains a choir vestry, meeting rooms for various church activities, a kitchen and toilets.

weedon
congregational church

The United Reformed Church now uses this former congregational church in Church Street. Its origins go back to the end of the 17th century, and by 1788 there was a joint congregation that covered Flore and Weedon Bec. Either in or about 1715, the Flore congregation was described as 'Independent', but by 1776 that at Weedon was considered to be 'Presbyterian'. In the same year, John Wesley, who was visiting the village, was not allowed to use the Parish Church and "accepted the offer of the Presbyterian Meeting-house".

The present building was erected in 1792, and registered as a place of worship a year later. The rubble walls and ashlar front support a hipped slate roof with a moulded eaves cornice. The east front has a segmental-arched doorway with fanlights that have been altered. The entrance has high pedimented canopies above, and the date 1792 can also be seen here.

Inside, the side walls, with their two bays, feature a double tier of segmental windows – semi-circular windows with a beam. In the rear wall there are two semi-circular arched windows, and behind it a low building which serves as a schoolroom and vestry. As with many chapels of this period, there are interior galleries situated on three sides of the building, the east one being built before the side ones, which were added in the 19th century. The pulpit is of a square design with raised panels. In the chapel there is a monument to Elizabeth, who died in 1824, the wife of Rev.

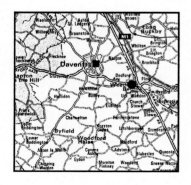

James Pinkerton. It is signed Whiting, North-ton (Northampton). Another monument, also with the same signature, is to the memory of the Rev. Joseph Gronow who, having been pastor for over 21 years, died in 1817. His wife, Mary Catherine (1816), and their two sons, Joseph Whitehead Gronow (1810) and William Hodgkinson Gronow (1821), are also remembered. The final interior memorial is to John Spencer who died in 1808, and takes the form of an oval tablet.

Outside in the front burial ground there are five stones, including those to James Barge (1822), his wife Anne (1821), Richard Smith (1807) and Sarah (1804).

108

welton
church of st martin

The church of St. Martin is at the highest end of this delightful, little changed and attractive Northamptonshire village. However, unlike many other nearby religious houses, it does not stand out, because it possesses a spireless tower. Built out of Northamptonshire stone, it naturally shows signs of weathering.

The church was originally a chapel to the church at Daventry, and given by William de Novo-Mercato, Lord of Welton. When the Bishop of Norwich made his general taxation in 1254, the church does not seem to have been endowed, but in 1291 it rated the vicarage at five marks, which, according to Bridges was the usual stipende for a capellane or curate. In the "sixteenth year of Elizabeth 1, John Marshe purchased the tythes, which at that time were called Ayre's-tythes", and which had previously belonged to the convent at Daventry.

St. Martin's, with its squat west buttressed tower, is in 14th century Decorated style, and lacks any intricate adornment, being crowned with a simple conical roof. The tower becomes narrower about one-third of the way from the top. Each side of the tower has a bell opening, and inside the substantial structure there is a ring of five bells, three of which date from 1629, one recast in 1825, and a further bell added to this peal by voluntary subscription in 1823. The bells continue to ring out across the village.

Entrance is either through the north or south doorways, both of which are in Decorated style. Once inside, there is a feeling not only of peace, but also of an airy and light building. The nave is made up of four bays of tall decorated arches supported by octagonal piers that have double chamfered arches. Although both of the aisles and the nave are quite tall, there is no clerestory. However, the white ceiling with its black beams give the building an air of spaciousness and light. During restoration work in the 19th century, new timbers were added to both aisle roofs, although the nave still retained some old beams. However, a fire in January 1997, thought to have been caused by an electrical fault, caused considerable damage

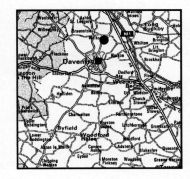

to the roof. Most of the damage was to the north side of the church, and to the nave, which left the church open to the sky. Some of the pews were also damaged, especially when burning timbers fell on them. The new roof is in keeping with the earlier design, and it is worth gazing upwards to take in some of the carving on the black beams.

All the windows in both the chancel and nave are of the Perpendicular period, and are well proportioned with their tall, elegant frames, and fitted with clear glass. There are three stained glass windows in the church, although a project is being considered to add either one or two new windows to mark the Millennium. By far the most distinctive is the east window behind the altar. There are four lights to this, all of which depict images of Jesus, in different situations, the left light featuring "Blessed are the pure in heart". Next to this, with the text, "Suffer little children to come unto me", Jesus has his hands on the heads of two children. The other two quotations are "Young man I say unto thee arise" and "Whosoever drinketh shall thirst again". Saints feature in the glass above accompanied by different texts.

> *There is an interesting story about the attractive ornately coloured floor in the sanctuary. One of the ladies who lived in the village did some work for a Russian prince, who also lived in Welton. As a thank you gift he gave her some malachite, which is turn was given to the church to be laid in the sanctuary floor. The green coloured stone forms a cross, and there are explicit instructions in a letter dated 1883 for cleaning the stone.*

The clear glass in the easterly windows on the north and south sides replaced earlier stained glass. It has been suggested that an earlier fire in the church affected these windows, although the effects did not reach this far. The window on the south side is in memory of Major General Sir Alexander Murray Tulloch KCB, and on the left to the Rev. John Alexander Clarke (1814–1860). The stained glass in the chancel above the choir stalls shows the return of the Prodigal son, Jesus healing, and a window to Sir William Hyde and Elizabeth Jane Pearson. It is thought that the two windows in the sanctuary with plain glass may have been of similar designs. Although it is not easy to see, the attractive and colourful west window in the tower is of St. Martin, the church's patron saint.

There is the usual piscina in the south wall of the sanctuary, but no sedilia is present. The typical priest's door is also here. The tub-shaped font is undoubtedly of great antiquity, although it is plain.

The church contains a number of memorials to its past memorable citizens, some of which take the form of wall tablets and date from the 1600s. Two of the oldest are to the memory of Thomas Frost on the east wall of north aisle, who died in 1699, and John Wafforne, who died early in the 18th century. That to the memory of Isaac Ashley is on the north wall close the organ, and is the work of William Cox of Northampton. Isaac died in 1732 and his wife in 1738. Below this, the small plaque with a cherub is in memory of their daughter, whose death occurred in 1779. A number of memorials to the Darnells are on the east wall of north aisle.

The statue of Jesus with the words "Feed my lambs. Feed my sheep" was given in memory of Edward Liddell, "Faithful parish priest". A brass plaque on the pillar of the easterly nave arch details those who carved the pulpit that was dedicated on St. Michael and All Angels day in 1899. The lectern and wrought iron work are also the work of local people. Earlier vicars are also remembered, including John Wainwright who died in 1778. Elisabeth Tebbutt, the daughter of the Rev. Francis Tebbutt, one of Welton's former curates, is commemorated by a wall tablet bearing the date 1842. Charles Liddell gave the almsbox just inside and to the east of the north door in 1899. A plaque on the east side of the south door is a memorial to the men of the parish who fell in the 1914–18 war.

In addition to the memorials already mentioned, there are a number of tablets in the church, and some of the most interesting are found on the chancel wall. That to John Clarke, who died in 1816, features a richly carved coffin with an obelisk above it. We are told that his death is "To the irreparable loss of the surrounding county". It also records his wife Mary, his "pious and affectionate relict". The striking Gothic tablet to John Plomer Clarke, on the north wall of the chancel, records his death in 1826. The wording on the memorial gives a long list of his works. Other members of the Clarke family are also remembered by a variety of tablets on the same wall. On the opposite wall there is a small plaque which commemorate Caroline and Major Guiseppe Trombone, two of the former inhabitants of Welton House. An interesting plaque to Mary Smith informs the reader that she died suddenly on a visit to Welton-place.

The first Vicar was one Albredus – *by prior and convent of Daventre* – who served between 1258 and 1269, and he was followed by John de Tilton, chaplain, on 2 November 1269.

Out in the well-kept churchyard, the view from the eastern end is across rolling Northamptonshire countryside where little has changed for centuries. The methods for gathering in the crops may be different, but local people have harvested the land and kept their cattle for generations. In the churchyard many former headstones have been placed along the north and east boundaries of the churchyard, and there are a number of table tombs on the south side of the church. The oldest headstones are found in the triangle formed by the gates on the north west side of the church. Two of these, to Thomas White and Elizabeth Cockerill, are from 1667. One memorial which stand in the same area of the churchyard – and which must undoubtedly be one of the saddest memorials to be found anywhere – is to six-year old John Hewitt, who is buried in the churchyard. According to the wording on his epitaph, he was the son of Peter and Eliz Hewitt of Rugby, and "he was lost (by neglect) Jan 16th 1806 in a field in this parish and was found on the 18th starved to Death in the 6th year of his Age."

The churchyard also has an elaborate tomb, with a Latin incription, to Robert Francis Burton of Churchill in the parish of Welton. He served throughout the Indian mutiny campaign, and died in 1903.

whilton
church of st andrew

Whilton is another of Northamptonshire's attractive and unspoilt villages located somewhat off the beaten track. The village has a history which goes back to Roman times – the former Roman town of Bannaventa has been located to the west of the parish, though people lived in the area prior to this. Bronze Age ancestors almost certainly used what is known as the Jurassic Way, an ancient trackway along which people travelled from the Humber to the Avon.

Today the peaceful village has a well cared for, delightful stone-built church dedicated to St. Andrew. Set in an attractive part of the village, it is surrounded by a number of older cottages. The base of the west tower is 13th century, with the west window having had some later work carried out. The filled in square-headed window towards the east side of the tower seems out of place in this position. The upper part of the tower is much later than the base, and owes its present form to rebuilding in 1769, with further work taking place a century or so later. It features four round bell-shaped openings, each of which has 'Y' shaped tracery.

Battlements adorn the top of the tower, which has an original ring of six bells, all cast in the London bellfoundry of Pack and Chapman in 1777. This bellfoundry also replaced the former two bells and priest's bell which hung in the tower in 1700. William Rose, who was patron at the time, gave these bells, and he was also responsible for meeting the bills for

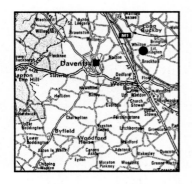

their installation. In 1994 the six bells were removed and melted down, and eight bells recast from them. The work was carried out by the Whitechapel bellfoundry, and when they were rehung, new fittings were also added. The heaviest of the bells is the tenor, weighing over 13cwt (660 kg).

A well maintained flagstone path, flanked by grass banks, leads to the relatively recently re-timbered south porch, and continues to the east into the nearby field – both paths are part of a public footpath system. From the churchyard there are superb views across the countryside, with the church sitting on the edge of village. Entrance to the church is through the south door, of modern construction. There is no north doorway.

The Church of St. Andrew was originally built in the 12th and 13th centuries, but most of the original building has all but been destroyed as successive generations have 'improved' the church. Work in the 18th century added to the nave and to upper sections of the tower. Other re-modelling has taken place to both the north and south arcades, and similar work has been carried out on the south door. Later restoration work was completed during 1957–58, when the lead covering the tower and nave was removed and replaced with copper.

Inside the church the stone walls have been plastered and covered with paint, but carefully executed in such a way that the stones around certain areas, including the windows and the arches, remain exposed. There are two aisles. The chancel, which was rebuilt between 1877–78, is higher than the nave, but still has some beams from an earlier era. The 13th century arches consist of two bays, and circular double chamfered piers capped with abaci (flat stones) support these. The small high windows are attractive, but allow relatively little light to enter.

The only distinctive stained glass is found in the east window, and is a clear representation of Christ nailed to the cross. Other figures shown include members of his family who grieve for him. The windows bear the inscription *The Blood of Christ cleanseth us from all sins*. In the upper panels of the window a scene depicts God on his throne surrounded by angels – the bright colours of the glass flood almost the whole of the chancel with light. The window was installed during the rebuilding of the chancel in 1878–79.

> *The first of Whilton's recorded Rectors was William de Pulteney, who served from 1333 to 1346. Unlike some other parishes, if Whilton suffered from the plague the rector did not appear to have succumbed, because Richard de Napton covered the plague period from 1346 to 1356.*

The reredos features a copy of Leonardi da Vinci's *The Last Supper*, executed in mosaic, which also spills over onto panels on either side, depicting wheat and a grapevine. The words "Do this in remembrance of me" also feature.

The interior furnishings are all Victorian, and include a sturdy font of relatively recent introduction. Just inside the south door, it is carved from stone and has a wooden oak cover enhanced with wrought iron tracery. The double-sided lectern, given in memory of the Rev. John Rose (1824–49), has also been carved from oak.

Although there are no elaborate free-standing monuments, the church possesses a range of memorial tablets. One on the south wall of the south aisle is in memory of John Murcott, a generous benefactor to charity. He was born in Whilton, and left sums of money to the poor of Harletone (Harlestone) and to "his native County Infirmary".

There are several memorials to members of the Rose family. These are to the Rev. Henry Rose (1849), positioned on the south wall of the south aisle, Rev. John Rose, Rector, who died in 1855, and Anne Rose (1829) and Christian Rose (daughter of Anne Rose – 1855) on the west wall of the south aisle. The monument to the Rev. William Lucus Rose (1814) on the north aisle of the north wall, makes interesting reading.

There is a well preserved architectural tablet on the south wall of the ringing chamber in memory of Richard Freeman (1749) and his wife Elizabeth. Either side has ionic pilasters – columns partly built into and partly projecting from the wall. The tablet has an urn at the top, the base taking the form of a roll of parchment, with turned up ends, referred to architecturally as 'cartouche'. Memorial slabs laid in the floor include those to Johannes Spateman (1749) and Elizabeth Spateman (1770) in the chancel.

The first of Whilton's recorded Rectors was William de Pulteney, who served from 1333 to 1346. Unlike some other parishes, if Whilton suffered from the plague the rector did not appear to have succumbed, because Richard de Napton covered the plague period from 1346 to 1356.

In the churchyard there are many old tombstone, including a number of tomb chests. The earliest of the gravestones is to Thomas Embry, who was a woolwinder, and who died in 1681. It is possible that either the stonemason or family got the name wrong, and it should be Emery! There are a number of other older gravestones leaning against the south wall of the church.

wolfhamcote
church of st peter

Like Fawsley, Wolfhamcote's St. Peter's Church – which is just in Warwickshire – has lost the parishioners which it once served. With no one to worship in the building, and no one to support its upkeep, it is not surprising that the deserted church became derelict, and with numerous attacks by vandals it languished in a forlorn state some mile or so off the busy A45, close to Braunston. Now, however, due to a great deal of restorative work, the building and its churchyard – which nestles behind a row of delightful lime trees – is back to something of its former glory. Although there are no nearby parishioners to warrant a regular service, the church is used from time to time for worship.

There is some confusion when talking about Wolfhamcote. The village is spelt 'Wolfhamcote', whereas the parish always has an additional 'p' – Wolfhampcote! At one time there were two medieval villages in the vicinity, Braunstonbury and Wolfhamcote, both of which became deserted. The two village sites are recorded as Scheduled Ancient Monuments. The former is thought to have been a manorial settlement, as opposed to a true village, but developed organically over a longer period of time. On the other hand, historians suggest that the settlement of Wolfhamcote, which is to the west of the relatively infant and gently flowing River Leam, probably had both a manor house and a mill. Archaeological finds suggest the site was occupied for about three hundred years from around the 12th to the 15th centuries.

The village, which by 15th to 17th century standards was probably quite large, dwindled in size, and was probably finally deserted in the 16th century. Historically the common fields were enclosed in 1501, and reports suggest that almost all the inhabitants had disappeared by 1517.

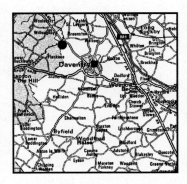

The church is reached along a private road from the A45, just before the canal bridge (coming from Daventry). It is easier to walk because the state of the track is hardly suitable for motor vehicles. If travelling by car, an alternative approach is from the Flecknoe direction along a public and better maintained road. The journey from Braunston passes over the River Leam, which marks the boundary between it and Northamptonshire. In spite of the disappearance of the village, the 14th century Church of St. Peter is still a consecrated building, now in the care of the Church Conservation Trust. Visitors who wish to view the interior can obtain keys from a nearby cottage – details near the church give the necessary information.

At first sight the church may appear deserted and forlorn, but there is a feeling of peace and tranquillity which the passage of time has not diminished. Standing on its own, with a cottage some 200 metres distant, the church is stranded between the embankments formed to take the now disued Great Central Railway and the Weedon to Leamington Railway, operated by North-Western Railways. The Oxford Canal also runs close by, but a new course for the original waterway was created in 1834, when the original line was straightened. It is between the church and the canal that the original village flourished.

The church gets its name from the first overlord to oversee the settlement, and the place name is derived from 'Ufelme's manor'. At the time of the Domesday survey it was in the hands of Turchill of Arden, who still owned lands after the Norman Conquest. The settlement consisted of 25 houses and a population of 100 people, with a priest to minister to their spiritual needs. Having passed through a succession of owners, including Christopher Hatton and Thomas Spenser, it eventually came into the possession of Richard Tibbits in 1794.

At first sight the church may appear deserted and forlorn, but there is a feeling of peace and tranquillity which the passage of time has not diminished. Standing on its own, with a cottage some 200 metres distant, the church is stranded between the embankments formed to take the now disused Great Central Railway and the Weedon to Leamington Railway, operated by North-Western Railways. The Oxford Canal also runs close by, but a new course for the original waterway was created in 1834, when the original line was straightened. It is between the church and the canal that the original village flourished.

It is assumed that there was a church on the site in earlier times, because the Domesday survey shows that the village had a priest. Now, though, nothing remains of an earlier structure, except perhaps for the font. The present church is quite large, and though unwise to make deductions from this, it would appear that the village in its heyday was probably of some substance.

Although the north-west tower, with its four bell openings, is squat, it is enhanced by a delightful battlement. It is here in the tower that the earliest part of the building remains, with the lower part of this structure dating from the 13th century. The tower only has two bells, a large one and a sanctus bell. In earlier times it was the Canons of St. Mary's in Warwick who installed a great bell, which bore the inscription *In multis annis resonat campana johannus* ("May John's bell for many years resound"). Dating back to about 1450, the bell was cast in London at the bellfoundry of John Sturdy, and he inscribed it with his sign, a cross formed from four fleurs-de-lis. Writing in *Church Bells of Warwickshire*, Reverend Tilley provides some information about these bells. He suggested that one of them had the inscription "Pack and Chapman of London", dated 1780 and made at Whitechapel. The bell cast by John Sturdy weighed between 18 and 19 cwt (approximately 2000 to 2200 lbs).

There is some suggestion that during the time at which the church was left derelict, one of the bells was stolen. However, both of the present bells were rehung during restoration, and Taylors of Loughborough were responsible for recasting them. The larger of the two bells now weighs 12 cwts (approximately 1400lbs).

Unlike many of the churches in this book, the tower at Wolfhamcote is situated to the north-west rather than the west, and is supported by stepped buttresses. There are two lines of windows: those in the belfry stage are tall and pointed; those above the line of the buttresses are much smaller. The date 1690 on the tower suggests that some building work took place at this time. Also given are the names of the vicar and church-warden, and in spite of erosion and the passage of time, these can still be seen on the battlements.

Inside the church is spacious and light due to the many clear windows. The glass has long since gone, the result of repeated attacks by vandals, so in its place the modern restorers have placed plastic sheeting, which in turn is also covered by wire netting to deter would-be attackers.

Both nave and south arcade are of the Decorated period, and are extremely wide. Prior to renovation this century, some work had been completed on the north windows in the 1600s. The arcades of chamfered arches that separate the aisles from the nave are held aloft on octagonal pillars, which feature rounded capitals. The northern arches are

believed to date from the 13th century; the rest from the 14th. At the west end of the north arcade there is only part of an arch, because when the tower was built it was constructed into the last bay of the northern aisle arch, resulting in a half arch. It is possible that further work was intended which would have changed the shape even more.

Entry into the ringing chamber is through a tall arch, but it is worth taking a look at the wheel from the larger bell. When a replacement became necessary, this was removed and fastened to the wall. The wooden screen that separates the north chapel from the north aisle is 14th century in origin, and delicate trefoil tracery can be seen in the upper part. The Clerkes and the Tibbits, former owners of the land, have their memorials here in the north chapel. They consist of texts that have been painted onto canvas. Here, too, is the customary piscina for the remains of the communion wine, and an aumbry in which the communion vessels were stored. The stone altar is a more recent addition to this part of the building.

The tall chancel arch is enhanced with carvings of heads on either side. These and other features survived attacks of vandalism that took pace when the building closed in 1950. Some parts did not, though, and the wooden stall rails have clerarly suffered. They were beyond saving, but damage to the 17th century communion table and carved sanctuary rails was repaired.

Various memorials can be found in this part of the church. There are several wall boards and wall tablets to various members of the Tibbits family, including Mary Tibbit, who later became Lady Hood, and who gave generously to the church. It was she who carried out the last alterations to the building. To erect a family vault for her husband, she enlarged the chancel and had a new east window put in, in Victorian Gothic style. This modernisation resulted in the loss of the old heraldic glass which had been in the church for centuries, and which showed the coats of arms of those families of noble birth who had had long associations with the village.

> *Lew Kershaw put into words the thoughts of many people in his 1986 poem, one verse of which reads*
>
> *Just a church and graveyard alone remain*
> *And a tithe barn which stored offerings of grain*
> *Yet of those who worked to fill this store? . . .*
> *Just eroded headstones – nothing more.*

The windows in the wall of the north aisle date from the reconstruction of the tower. One is from the 15th century, and the other a copy but produced 400 years later. The 14th century windows in the south aisle have survived for almost 600 years, and still keep their impressive and exquisite reticulated tracery.

In the floor there are gravestones to various members of the Raynsford family, and a small brass tablet dated 1687 remembers the wife of the Rev. Thomas Benyon, vicar of the parish.

The origins of the hexagonal pulpit, with its inlays of light wood, is not certain. It may have been produced for another church, but was bought by Lady Wood for St. Peter's. The monuments set in the floor close to the pulpit were placed there in memory of George Tibbits, Michael Clerke and the Rev. Thomas Geldart, a former vicar. The royal coat of arms of Queen Anne, which is above the chancel, has been restored.

If, like many other churches, St. Peter's has no fine stained glass, one of its treasures must surely be pieces of wooden furniture which grace the building. The simple roughly hewn benches, created from oak, and either of late 14th or early 15th centuries in origin, give a clear indication of the furniture in earlier churches. One of the earlier pieces of furniture to survive is the 12th century communion rail that has twisted balusters. One of the most attractive features in the church is the superb 14th century screen in the north chapel.

Upwards, too, in the roof there are some beams which have survived the onslaught of a variety of wood-boring insects since they became part of the church in its early medieval days. During reconstruction of the chancel roof in 1848, it was possible to re-use some of the materials, the earliest of which was from the 15th century. Standing in the chancel, it is worth taking a look at the roof, of Tudor origin.

The tub font, a survival from the earlier Norman church, is in a delicate state, and has been restored by covering it with cement to preserve it and retain its shape.

Outside in the churchyard, attached to the east end of the chancel in a walled area, is a large 18th century Gothic mausoleum to the Tibbit family.

woodford halse
church of st mary the virgin

The large, and continuously expanding village, which is situated less than two miles from the ever-increasingly busy A361, was once even more important at the time of the railways. The Church of St. Mary stands close to some of the terraced houses that once provided homes for the railway workers. Close by is the village's community centre, which originally served as the village school. Over the centuries this stalwart building has seen many changes.

It was built from warm local sandstone, which weathers badly, and a great deal of restoration work had to be carried out in 1878. However, this was not the first time, and reports between 1631 and 1637 made various references to damaged stained glass, seats in the chancel ("some are gone and some are loose") – and interestingly "Mr Catesby's and Mr Standish's seats are too high"! Early in the 18th century, work was carried out on the roof, two churchwardens being responsible for the repairs, as noted on a plaque in the belfry.

However, major re-building work was necessary in the 19th century because the original church had fallen into a state of disrepair, and such was the state of the building that it virtually needed complete refurbishment to bring it back to its original glory. As more and more railway workers poured into the expanding village, it was felt that the church needed to be there for them.

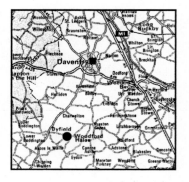

The simple, yet not unattractive, Decorated west tower had stood sentinel over succeeding generations of local people since it first rose in about 1300. A single bell opening, with its distinctive Y-tracery, graces each side of the tower. The west window also exhibits the same features. The tower houses a ring of six bells, the earliest four from 1613. The tenor is undated, and the treble, together with the priest's bell, date from 1975, when the original ring of five bells was increased to six with the addition of a priest's bell. When the framework was assessed it was discovered that most of the wood was rotten, and the bells had remained silent for many year. To enable them to ring again, it was decided to replace the existing frame with a metal one at the same time as the sixth bell was added by the Loughborough bellfoundry of John Taylor and Co. A crack developed in the fourth when it was being rung in 1983, and because of its age it would not have been possible to have it recast. Instead, the crack was expertly welded, and the bell was soon back in tune. Thomas North made an interesting discovery about Woodford Halse's bells, and in his book *The Bells of Northamptonshire* (1878), he notes "This is the only instance of a complete ring of four alphabet bells I have met with".

The church is reached along a pleasant path, flanked on either side by flower beds, making the approach particularly attractive during the summer. The churchyard is extensive, but in spite of its size, most of it is well-kept. Some of the overgrown areas are especially important for wildlife.

Inside the church, the nave has two aisles, each of which has arcades made up of four arches. In the north aisle the arches, with their single chamfers, are borne on circular piers, with their octagonal abaci. Although this particular arcade dates from the 13th century, one of the capitals has an interesting Norman scallop decoration around it. In contrast, the south arcade has octagonal piers that feature double chamfered arches, and is probably from the 14th century. The clerestory has four windows in each side; those on the south have the same designs, but those on the north have a variety of outlines. In the nave the windows have Victorian tracery, but it is possible that some part of one in the south wall dates from medieval times.

In 1871 the poor state of part of the building, including the tower, was such that it was feared people might be injured, especially during the winter should heavy snow settle on the badly damaged roof. The church was closed and services held in the nearby village school. Enough funds had been raised by the beginning of January 1878, and the old church was pulled down. Reference had been made over the centuries to the Lady Chapel, but this had disappeared; it was during this rebuilding work that it was rediscovered. As with many churches, Woodford had had its walls decorated with medieval paintings, but these had been covered over. Of the small areas discovered, it was not possible to distinguish what was depicted, with the exception of St. Christopher, the patron saint of travellers, who can also be also be seen at Ashby St. Ledger. Perhaps the most important discovery, unearthed in the south aisle, were ancient foundations from a very much earlier church. Apart from some examples of herringbone brickwork, a number of skeletons and single bones were also unearthed. Further skeletal remains turned up when the south pillars were removed, suggesting that these had been buried prior to the building of the last church on the site.

The chancel also came under the influence of the Victorian restorers. To carry out the work it was necessary to raise £3000, the committee setting themselves a target of five years. However, unlike many churches, St. Mary's was carefully planned, and the restoration is in keeping with the earlier building. So well has the old blended in with the new that the Victorian influence is almost impossible to detect, and visitors may be forgiven for thinking they are in an original medieval building.

The chancel also came under the influence of the Victorian restorers. To carry out the work it was necessary to raise £3000, the committee setting themselves a target of five years. However, unlike many churches, St. Mary's was carefully planned, and the restoration is in keeping with the earlier building. So well has the old blended in with the new that the Victorian influence is almost impossible to detect, and visitors may be forgiven for thinking they are in an original medieval building.

The wide variety of stained glass is also largely Victorian, and is a particularly attractive feature of the church. Of the older remains, the octagonal font is thought to date from the 1660s. There are some interesting benches in both the chancel and nave – those in the choir stall with poppy-head decoration are the oldest.

The priests were originally known as Rectors, and the first of these was Richard de Bluby (1320–1328). They changed to Vicars during the 14th century, and Walter de Askley (1328–1329) was the first.

An interesting and extremely old sculpture, of which only the bottom part remains, is in the nave's east wall. One of the earliest monuments in the church is a brass beneath the chancel floor, now covered by the aisle carpet. In memory of Nicholas Stafford, a former vicar who died in 1400, the figure measures 20 in (50cm) in length.

A recumbent effigy was discovered close to the chancel's north wall during 19th century restoration work, when a number of excavations were made for the new building. The figure carved on the stone is thought to be of Maud Holland, Lady of Woodford Halse Manor during the early 14th century. It rests in a specially created tomb recess on the north wall of the chancel. Close by but higher up is a memorial to Catherine Knightley, erected by Giles Knightley, who is buried in the same place. In the opposite wall there is a priest's door, and close by a brass to Sergt Albert Smith who died during the First World War.

The Lady Chapel was restored to mark the centenary of the building of the new church. To make way for it, some pews were removed, and the items that are included have come from parishioners. A squint, used by those siting in the pews to see the altar, is also visible in the Lady Chapel.

The latest addition to the church is an extension in memory of Margaret Allen, consisting of a kitchen and toilets. The plaque indicates that the extension was "built primarily with a legacy left to the church by Margaret Allen, a faithful worshipper until her death on 14 June, 1987".

Outside, the gargoyles are of interest as is a scratch dial at the east of the church between the last two windows. Recently, the county council listed some 117 memorials in the churchyard. There is a mixture of chest tombs and headstones, all covering the period from the late 17th century to the 19th century. The memorials include chest tombs (1762, 1806 and late 18th century) and headstones, ranging in date from 1695 (headstone with winged hourglass) to 1708 (with cherub's head). The war memorial to those who fell in both world wars is on the west side of the path, just inside the gate.

woodford halse
moravian church

During 1787 some inhabitants from Woodford Halse had been attending Moravian churches in nearby villages. In this year William Hunt, a local farmer, who had also been attending worship, started to teach, and in 1788 it was decided to apply for a licence for a house meeting. This was refused, until finally approved in 1796, and a group of Moravians began meeting in Woodford Halse. The Woodford group was recognised as a Congregation of the Brethren. Two years later in 1798 work began on the chapel, together with a house for the minister. This was completed the next year. Each member of the congregation was responsible for the work. A group from the London congregation had donated the Chelsea organ. In 1799 when the chapel formerly opened, a minister moved into the adjoining house.

Alterations and reorientation took place in 1828, and further work was carried out in 1875. Originally the south-west side had two doorways. Above these were small windows, and between these was a taller window. Alterations in 1875 led to the replacement of these, which were substituted with three-segmented arched windows. This brought some kind of uniformity to the building, because these newly installed windows also matched the windows of similar design in the opposite wall. At this time the entrance to the north-west was removed, and a large porch added to the west side of the building. The present organ came to the church in 1880, provided as the result of a donation from a Mr Malin of Philadelphia.

With extra workers moving into Woodford with the coming of the railway, the Moravians felt that their modest building was not large enough. A new chapel was begun early in 1906, and completed in October of the same year. It was dedicated by a large congregation attending the services.

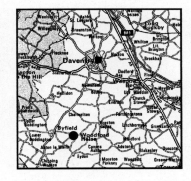

The original building is a brick structure sitting on a stone plinth, and a slate roof provides protection from the weather. The minister's house, which is two-storeys high, is at the south east end.

In the original building the pulpit stood against the north-east wall, but it was relocated 1828, when it was placed against the south east wall. At the same time the north west gallery was installed. The gallery, with a barely noticeable projecting centre, is held on two octagonal posts. The circular stained glass window above the altar shows the Lamb of God, and bears the words *Vicit Noster Eum Sequamur*, which according to the Moravian translation becomes "Our Lamb is conquered – let us follow Him".

There is a burial ground behind the chapel and an identical flat numbered tablet marks individual burial positions. This system is used because the Moravians believe that everyone is equal in the eyes of the Lord.